Sanctuary
of Your
Own

About the Author

Caroline was raised in Grosse Pointe Farms, Michigan. As a child, she loved taking long walks through the tree-lined streets of her neighborhood, imagining how various home-owners might have decorated their inner sanctums.

She holds a PhD in Luso-Brazilian Studies, has taught literature and language at Brown, Pittsburgh, and Colorado universities, and worked for many years as a master inter-cultural trainer and assessor. Among her leisure pursuits are jogging, gardening, herb crafting, and manufacturing aro-matherapy products, which she sells in her online business, Caroline Dow Products.

She also writes both nonfiction and fiction books, eighteen of which have been published to date. In the realm of fiction, she writes historical mysteries set in seventeenth-century Mexico City featuring as a sleuth a fictionalized version of Sor Juana, a real nun from those times. She also writes a modern crime fiction series set in Colorado, where the main character is a young Latina Spanish professor.

Caroline makes her home in Boulder, Colorado, where she and her family enjoy remodeling their historic home. This sanctuary has received an award of merit from Historic Boulder for a compatible addition, has been on the Boulder Historic Homes Tour, and was featured in an intercultural training film and a crime fiction novel.

Visit her online at both www.carolinedowbooks.com and https//etsy.com/shop/CarolineDowProducts.

Sanctuary *of* Your Own

Create a Haven Anywhere
for Relaxation & Self-Renewal

Caroline Dow

Llewellyn Publications
Woodbury, Minnesota

FIRST EDITION
First Printing, 2019

Book design by Rebecca Zins
Cover design by Shannon McKuhen

Llewellyn Publications is a registered trademark
of Llewellyn Worldwide Ltd.

The Library of Congress Cataloging-in-Publication Data is pending.

ISBN 978-0-7387-6242-5

Llewellyn Publications
A Division of Llewellyn Worldwide Ltd.
2143 Wooddale Drive
Woodbury, MN 55125-2989
www.llewellyn.com

Printed in the United States of America

To my friends and colleagues who graciously gave of their time and ideas in interviews about their sanctuaries and who helped me fill in the blank spaces with wit and wisdom. May your sacred spaces help roll you to glory!

Contents

Acknowledgments

I'd like to thank the following people for consenting to be interviewed about their personal sanctuaries. Their thoughtful and enlightening responses made valuable contributions to this book. They are: Hyman and Nancy Brown, Thora Chinnery, Poppy Copeland, Alicia Cristofano, John Dow, Nancy Downie, Ellen Haynes, Christiane Howard, Sherri Jennings, Lawrie Kimbrough, Debra Livingston, Sara Martinelli, Frederick Mayberry, Frank Miller, Tania Petrulius, Shauna Sandstead-Corona, and Barbara Steiner. And I especially want to thank my editor Amy Glaser, whose enthusiasm for this project has cheered me on.

A Home in Your Heart

*Your sacred space is where you can
find yourself again and again.*
Joseph Campbell

Many of us dream of a personal haven, a retreat from the whirlwind of our busy daily lives. A safe place tucked away from the stresses of work, traffic, family, the never-ending to-do list, and other demands. A refuge where no one can intrude and where we can feel free to just be ourselves. A retreat where we can engage in creative pursuits such as a favorite hobby or journaling. Or simply a nonjudgmental space for self-development, meditation, prayer, or contemplation.

If this description fits your desire, you can stop dreaming now and begin carving out a sanctuary of your own. This sacred space, which doesn't necessarily refer to religion, is a place that is sacrosanct to you and you alone. The world abounds with space; it exists all around us, even in our minds. To create your haven, you must start by both harnessing the power of your perceptions and your intentions to realize your dream.

You can locate your sanctuary almost anywhere. Your entire home can become a consecrated realm or you may focus on one room or corner. Your special haven may find a home in your garden, on your patio or balcony, at a park, by an ocean or lake, or deep within a forest or desert. You can construct a mini sanctuary at work, in your car, and even in your hotel room when you're traveling. The settings are as limitless as your imagination and circumstances.

Boundaries

Personal space naturally entails boundaries. You erect these physical, mental, or emotional fences around you to exclude unwanted intrusions. Yet boundaries also keep in what you hold to be sacred. The things you choose to surround yourself with speak to your individual personality, preferences, family background—even your values and attitudes toward life.

A sanctuary is a place where one can withdraw and spend time alone. It also can be a designated area to share quiet moments with someone special or celebrate with those you love. If you envision your haven from this perspective, you'll see that you can socialize or exchange ideas with others in this relaxed environment. A dining room filled with family and friends is as much a hallowed precinct as a meditation room or altar. In this way, a boundary becomes a frontier for exploring and interacting with others' personal spaces. You may even discover ways to expand or reimagine your sacred space. You can adapt ideas you've discovered in other people's homes, offices, or personal retreats to reflect your own refuge. In this way, you create a synergistic space greater than the sum of its parts.

About This Book

In this book I show how to put together a haven to bring balance, serenity, and joy into your life. I discuss ways you can use this space to express your individuality, personal interests, cultural background, and spirituality. The subjects covered include ways to design intimate spaces in the home, at work, in the garden, on the patio or balcony, or in the great outdoors. You'll even find suggestions on how to bring nature indoors to you. I also consider transitory spaces like your car or a room where you're spending the night away from your home base. Together we tackle the task of how to simplify your sanctuary by getting rid of clutter and downsizing. If you live in a small space, I devote a chapter to those unique challenges. And I pinkie swear that you won't need to put in an extraordinary effort or spend a small fortune to achieve amazing results.

I've included interviews conducted with my insightful friends and colleagues about how they've arranged their unique spaces. I also tell anecdotes drawn from my own successes and failures to inform and, hopefully, inspire you. From time to time, I offer a meditation and share some delicious recipes to help you relax in your retreat. The appendix contains useful information on botanicals, flowers, gemstones, totems, trees, and the significance of numbers to help you personalize your space.

A Sanctuary for All Life's Stages

For almost all my life, I've been observing how and why people create and use their private spaces. One of my earliest memories involves moving with my parents to a gray shoebox of a house in Cleveland, Ohio, where the interior walls were painted a depressing shade of army green.

The first thing Mom and Dad did was repaint the living room a sunny yellow and the tiny bedrooms in rose and turquoise. In those days, nobody—and I mean nobody—painted rooms in those hues. Everyone thought my parents had weird home decorating tastes, but our family didn't mind. We enjoyed our bright, chirpy little house because the sunny paint on the walls seemed to make our little box twice as big as any of the other identical tract houses on the block. This book's chapter on color may give you suggestions on how you can enliven your own space using similar techniques.

Later, I became an intercultural trainer, where I helped executives and their families from multinational corporations adjust to living assignments abroad. In my job I was lucky to get the opportunity to see how people from other places around the world design their sanctuaries. In this book I share many tips garnered from other cultures so you, too, may learn from other peoples' sanctuary solutions.

Last year I was diagnosed with an aggressive cancer. Between the emergency operation and starting chemotherapy, my husband helped me repaint and redecorate my home office to use as a meditation space. I'm sure the emotional comfort I derived from that room helped put me into the complete remission that my doctors termed "a miracle." Your emotional needs may not be as intense as mine, but I hope you'll benefit from some of the ideas I've put forth for creating a bedroom shrine and meditation space.

You don't need a magic wand to transform any space into a haven. Everything hinges on the stimulation and interplay of your five senses. Just familiarize yourself with some facts about the senses and how they relate to your sanctuary. Then engage your sense of fun, and you'll be a pro in no time.

Now I invite you to grab a latte or a cup of tea, settle into a quiet corner, and join me on a sensual journey of space exploration.

one

Your Senses and You

One way to create a safe, congenial environment for relaxation, reflection, and renewal is to heighten your perceptions by reaching deep into your subconscious to stimulate your five senses. The interplay of hearing, smell, touch, taste, and sight can orchestrate a symphony of delight for you in your sacred space. In this chapter we'll explore some basic principles associated with the functions of the senses and show what you can do to enhance your sensory perceptions in your sanctuary. In later chapters I'll apply these principles to specific situations.

Hearing

Hearing is one of the easiest senses to incorporate into your hallowed space. Sound, whether it manifests as a bubbling fountain, a loved one's voice, or a catchy tune, can be a potent stimulant. Music, in particular, invigorates us by reaching to the inner depths of our beings, communicating experiences richly layered in meaning. A beloved song from a favorite musical can gladden your heart. A favorite oldie may evoke poignant memories.

Listening to music in your sacred space can make it easier to calm your body, emotions, and mind, putting you more in tune, so to speak, with higher states of consciousness. After all, music is a well-known device used to break the ice at parties or meetings, where people unfamiliar with each other come together. We often hear music playing in the background at grocery stores and shopping malls because retailers know that by creating a relaxed and happy mood, shoppers will be more receptive to buying their merchandise.

Music also makes an ideal tool for learning because it teaches us in subliminal ways by bypassing the intellect. You probably still remember the words and melodies of many nursery rhymes and songs you learned effortlessly in childhood. If you're going to use your sanctuary as a place for learning, it can be helpful to have music playing in the background, especially if you don't find it distracting. Choose whatever kind moves you—classical, country, hip-hop, jazz, reggae, rock. Simply turn on your device and enjoy the familiar sounds while you study or contemplate an issue you want to resolve.

If you find that background music makes your mind wander, try introducing bells, chimes, crystal bowls, a tabletop waterfall, or a percussion instrument. Banging on a drum or shaking a tambourine or pair of maracas can be more restorative than any medicinal tonic, especially when you're feeling frustrated. If you live in a suburban or rural area, consider opening the window to absorb nature sounds. At first you might not notice them over the din of lawn mowers, passing cars, or children at play in nearby yards. As your thoughts settle down, the serene sounds you want to hear will emerge. Many city dwellers find the hum of urban life outside their windows equally comforting.

Smell

When people start assembling their sanctuaries, they sometimes neglect this important sense. Maybe that's because compared to other animals, we humans are lightweights when it comes to our sniffers: 98 percent of the smells we experience never reach our conscious minds. Still, smell remains one of our most acute senses. Scent molecules travel directly through the most primitive part of the brain, the limbic system, to the subconscious mind, where odors affect our emotions. This is why people react strongly, and often irrationally, to smells.

Memories of our fundamental life experiences are intimately linked to our sense of smell. While on an autumn walk after a late season rain, you may experience bliss when you inhale the earthy odor rising from the damp leaves crushed underfoot; this same scent may sadly remind another person on the same walk of a wrecked relationship or of a relative who passed away at that time of year. As you plan your sacred space, you might want to think about how to incorporate into it the aromas you associate with your favorite season to conjure luscious scent memories and stimulate your imagination.

The primal emotions from odors help us access a well-spring of vivid images and associations, which can bring about perceptions that are often more direct, clear, and significant than conscious thoughts. These will aid your self-understanding and self-realization.

Beyond forming a bridge for communication with your subconscious, certain fragrances help you rest and regroup. This is probably one reason the clean smell of lavender has been used for centuries to scent bed linens. A fragrance like eucalyptus can clear your head and infuse your body's tissues with new vitality. Aromatherapists work with essential oils to help cure patients of physical and psychological ills. They claim that aromas can have a restorative effect on the body.

There are many ways to add scent to your sanctuary. You can use an aromatherapy diffuser, potpourri, scent beads, sachets, or incense. Incense can exert such a powerful influence that I devote an entire chapter later in this book to showing how to enjoy it and even how to make your own personally crafted formulas. If, for whatever reason, you can't tolerate perfumes, I encourage you to engage in a little bit of experimentation. Thousands of aromas are out there just waiting to be explored. Begin with the lighter, cleaner fragrances such as the aforementioned lavender and eucalyptus, or lemon or rosemary, which evaporate quickly. Steer clear of the heavier, darker, longer-lasting scents such as amber, musk, oakmoss, and patchouli.

Touch

Imagine how dreary life would be if you were deprived of your sense of touch. You'd never enjoy the caress of a loved one, feel your pet's soft fur, or thrill to the warmth of a sandy beach on your bare feet followed by the cool caress of wetness lapping around your toes as you skip into the water. All contact with the physical world around you would vanish. Helen Keller, who lost her vision and hearing as a baby, was finally reached through her sense of touch. The moment she realized touch could communicate words and concepts to her, the entire universe expanded beneath her fingers.

To stimulate your sense of touch in your sanctuary, decorate it with a variety of textures, from satin to silk and velvet to Berber wool. Embroidered pillows, colorful throw rugs, and cloth wall hangings or tapestries will create a feast for your sense of touch as well as for your eyes. Leafy and succulent plants also add texture.

One kind of texture you may not have thought of for your sanctuary is provided by wood. Wood comes in many forms, from a solid oak table to bamboo screens to indoor trees such as miniature Meyer lemons or potted palms. In later chapters I'll talk about varieties of woods and living plants and how you can use their subtly different textures to your advantage.

Taste

As anyone who's ever caught a cold can tell you, taste and smell are almost inseparable. When your nose is stuffed up, your food tastes like sawdust. You've probably heard a million times the saying "You are what you eat." Usually, the speaker hopes to convince the listener to swallow something for better health or to change a bad eating habit. I don't imagine many of us pause to consider the deeper meaning of these words. As we eat and drink, we not only change physically; we also nourish our bodies with a substance that transforms our minds and spirits. Our ancestors realized this fact and handed their wisdom down to us in various food-and-drink-related traditions and rituals. The practice of toasting the good health, well-being, and prosperous future of a bride and groom is an example.

One way to add taste to your sanctuary is by using fragrances that remind you of food. You might choose to burn a cinnamon-scented candle or incense either in your sanctuary or at the dinner table. Although this bark has a spicy scent, the energy it imparts is considered peaceful. Use cinnamon to bless a room or generate an environment conducive to social interaction. Cinnamon's aroma is also indicated as an aid to intuition, self-development, inspiration, improved memory, knowledge, and wisdom. Seems you can't go wrong with cinnamon!

Another way to use taste in your sanctuary is to decorate with colors evocative of favorite foods, like cherry red, avocado green, or mellow banana yellow. I'll tell you straight out that I hate doing laundry. When I moved to my current house, the large basement laundry room with its cheap dark brown paneling and bare overhead light bulb felt so depressing. I knew that if I didn't remedy the situation right away, my family would have to live forever more in dirty clothes! Without much money, I had to be inventive.

First I installed inexpensive overhead lighting. Then I applied sweat equity and covered that dreadful brown paneling with pretty peach-colored paint. For an attractive contrast and to hide the dirt, I painted the molding navy blue. What a difference! By tradition, the Chinese consider the peach to be a fruit of immortality. In China the peach blossom season is also thought to be the most auspicious time for marriage. So by just changing the lighting and painting the walls, I now have a space that lifts my potentially dejected mood on laundry day and focuses my mind and feelings on love, contentment, and long-lasting good health.

Occasionally I like to eat and drink in my sanctuary. Teas in winter and smoothies in summer help me kick back, mull over the day's events, or jump-start my day. I try to use ingredients in my recipes that relate in some way to whatever I'm going to do there. For example, I drink a ginseng infusion spiked with a pinch of lemon balm to energize me, white tea with a drop of vanilla and some honey to relax me, and a favorite mocha blend spiced with cinnamon to fuel my creative juices.

Laura, a fellow author, also includes taste in her sanctuary by drinking a cup of herbal tea every time she sits down to write. She's found that the little ritual of preparing, smelling, and tasting the tea prompts her subconscious mind to engage in writing mode. It's also a signal to her husband and children not to disturb her while she's working.

Sight

Without our sense of sight, we would be plunged into a confusion of never-ending darkness. Practically everyone understands that light affects us physically and psychologically. In summer, when the lazy days stretch out for hours on end, we feel vibrant and alive and enjoy outdoor activities, including lots of socializing. In winter, as the sun withdraws its light and warmth, we tend to spend more time inside and enjoy solitary pursuits such as reading in bed.

Although we know these things about light, we don't always realize that color also affects us profoundly. To create a harmonious sacred space, you need to know about some of these effects. The therapeutic abilities of color—including its power to soothe and stimulate—have been known, at least intuitively, almost since humankind began keeping records. Color has been used for healing by cultures as diverse as ancient Egyptians, Native Americans, Celts, Asians, Greeks, Persians, and Teutonic peoples. In the next chapter we'll delve into the exciting world of color and learn how you can use it to enhance your sanctuary. For now, let's concentrate on how to get the right combination of harmonious sense stimulators into your space.

This takes some planning and experimentation, but it's not as difficult as you might think. Your intuition will do a lot to guide you. Really! Let me give you an example. As you read this story, I'd like you to contemplate the ways you'll artfully combine the senses into your haven.

Last year I volunteered as a guide for our town's historic house tour. The home where I worked was a traditional Craftsman-style structure built to look like an English Tudor, with stone and stucco walls and lots of rich, dark walnut and oak paneling. Since our tour takes place during the winter holidays, the weather is often cold and snowy. But on that bright, windless day, the sun shone in a cerulean sky and the temperature rose to a toasty sixty degrees.

It seemed that everybody, once they visited the house, lingered on the back patio to rest on the wrought-iron outdoor porch furniture. This presented a disconcerting situation for volunteers, who needed to keep traffic flowing. Every so often, one of us had to step outside and remind people there were other houses to see and if they stayed too long, they might cause a bottleneck. Reluctantly, visitors eventually moved on.

On my break I decided to take a good look at the patio to discover what made it so inviting. It was nestled into a corner formed by a couple of rough but warm sandstone walls, softened by creeping green English ivy. Slate covered the ground. Five Celtic knots, four small corner ones and a large central knot bounded by circles, were sandblasted into the stone that covered the ground. This motif fit well with the Craftsman style.

A plaster fountain shaped like a big grinning frog burbled whimsically near the casual furniture groupings. Froggy was painted green and dressed like a butler, offering a lily pad instead of a salver. The homeowners had erected a five-foot live spruce tree in a planter and placed it on a low stone boundary ledge. The tree's miniature lights and silver and gold ornaments glittered like fairy lights in the sunshine. Potted poinsettias amassed on tables and on ledges provided more splashes of color.

I sat staring at the postcard view of the Front Range of the Rockies to the southwest. The sun warmed my face as I listened to the singing fountain and birds chirping in the background. For some minutes, I drank in the fresh, tangy aroma of the evergreens surrounding me. Mesmerized, I watched the squirrels scamper over the damp, earth-fragranced lawn in search of late fall nuts and seeds. No wonder the visitors didn't want to leave this haven! This patio stimulated all my senses in such a cheerful but low-key way that even I had a hard time dragging myself back to my post. I wondered whether the homeowners consciously realized what they had created. They probably just combined elements in a way that pleased them.

Smudging Ritual to Cleanse and Purify Your Haven

Most cultures over time have devised little rituals to cleanse and purify their immediate surroundings, the places where they feel most safe but perhaps at the same time most vulnerable to unwanted intrusions. In ancient times the motive may have been to chase away demons and ghosts and protect against ill winds or enemies of a more physical origin. Today many people, especially when moving to a new home, still like to give the place a thorough cleaning, for hygienic purposes and to spiritually purify their new environment.

Here's a simple ritual for you to perform to cleanse and sanctify your haven. You can do it for a space as large as your entire home, as small as an altar, or for any size space in between. The rite, based on Native American clearing and protection methods, requires minimum ingredients and minimum fuss. All you need is a small porcelain bowl, a book of matches, a fairly large feather of any kind, and a smudge stick.

Different herbs can be used for smudging. The most common is sage. It's convenient, since over one thousand species grow worldwide, and it's thought to be the most effective purifier. You can find sage smudges almost anywhere in herb stores, even in some groceries, pharmacies, and gift shops. Sage (*Salvia* genus) is an evergreen bush of the mint family that can grow waist-high. The grayish-green leaves exude a somewhat astringent menthol scent. This plant blooms with little bluish-violet flowers. You may be familiar with sage as a standard ingredient in Thanksgiving turkey stuffing. Although all kinds of sage make equally effective cleansers, desert sage, also called purple sage (*S. Dori*), is the most ubiquitous. Personally, I prefer white sage (*S. apiana*), also called sacred sage, for its lighter, airier fragrance.

If you don't care for the fragrance of sage, there are other options. Cedar (*Thuja occidentalis*), for one, is highly touted to drive away negativity (as well as moths). Yerba santa (*Eriodictyon californicum*), a botanical of the US West Coast and

Mexico, is used by Native Americans to help assuage coughs and colds. This herb will protect the borders of your space and sanctify the area. Sweetgrass (*hierochloe odorata*), a sweetly scented grass, invites positive energy and is great to use as a consecration smudge after purification.

To perform the rite, first take all the ingredients outside so random sparks don't land on the carpet or furniture. Light the smudge, get it going, then blow it out and place it upside down in the bowl. Now go to your sanctuary; start at the back of the house, room, or altar. Hold the bowl with the smudge in one hand. Take the feather in your other hand and gently waft it over the smoke that should be emitting from the smudge by now. The operative word here is "gently." You don't want any sparks to fly out of the bowl. As you walk through the area fanning with the feather, repeat over and over:

All that's wrong
Begone, begone!
All that's good
Come flowing in.

Smudge every corner of your sanctuary, including windows and doors. When you reach the front, place the smudge and bowl outside. Take some water and douse it enough to know the smudge is out. You can hang the used smudge over the threshold to your dwelling or sanctuary to help block negativity from entering. And best of all, after the smudge has dried out, you can use it again whenever you feel your space needs a refresher.

two

Color Your World

Now that we've made sense of the senses, let's move on to take a look at color and how you can use it to enhance your experience in your sanctuary. In this chapter I can only paint the surface of this vast subject, but if what I say stimulates your curiosity, I've included a resources section at the back of the book for you to deepen your knowledge.

Coloring Your Sacred Space

Before you start running around with color swatches and sample paints in different hues, let's spend a few minutes talking about some ideas surrounding basic colors. Color is an exciting concept; without it, our world would be a pretty drab place.

Here are some general points to consider when adding color to your sanctuary. You probably have a favorite color you tend to overuse. If you notice that your space is getting too monochromatic, try including a complementary hue for balance. Complementary colors are pairs of colors that, when placed next to each other, show a strong but pleasing contrast.

An example of two opposite colors, as they are sometimes also called, is blue and orange. This is why life vests and rafts are orange; they contrast with the blue sea and can be seen easily. Other traditional opposite hues are red/green and yellow/purple. Possible pairs that other color experts who use a different color scale agree on are red/cyan, green/magenta, and blue/yellow. Decorating with these blends creates a comfortable environment both at home and in the workplace and produces a sense of completeness.

When painting adjacent surfaces, I suggest you avoid using primary colors together. These three true colors—red, yellow, and blue—from which other colors derive, do well together in a child's room because they exude an exciting, primitive aura. You can take advantage of this feeling if you're going for a primeval look, but be aware that the initial excitement soon wears thin. In fact, some people, especially those of nervous or delicate dispositions, can be adversely affected by the combination of primary colors when they spend too much time surrounded by them. So if you are striving for harmony and balance in your private place, or if you are a retailer or boss who wants to avoid a constant employee turnover, I recommend you give primary color combinations a miss.

The Color Palette

Our relationship with color is complex, and we all make different associations depending on our preferences and experiences. Still, there are some general concepts that can be applied to describe each hue. To simplify matters, here are some short color synopses for you to refer to as you plan your haven. I'll begin at the red end of the spectrum and work my way to the blue end. Afterward, I'll offer suggestions on how to use color in your space to enhance good health.

Red

This virile color brims with energy, strength, warmth, and physicality. An intense, passionate hue, red initially stimulates the senses. When people are placed in a red room, their reaction times are measured as 12 percent quicker than in rooms of other colors. It's no wonder this color is chosen for stop signs, stop lights, and fire equipment, yet the initial energizing effect tends to subside over time and be replaced by a calming influence. If you spend much time in a red room, both your pulse rate and blood pressure are likely to drop. Red is also thought to spark creativity and initiate action on projects. However, because red is such a strong stimulant, it can also engender feelings of aggressiveness and defiance.

If you're drawn to red, consider painting at least one wall of your sanctuary this color to facilitate meditation. Perhaps this is one reason many Buddhist temples make liberal use of red in their decor, and the Chinese consider it to be a fortunate color.

Red can uplift a mood. If you're recovering from a long illness or otherwise feel stressed or energy-depleted, consider drinking red-colored tea in your sanctuary. It will strengthen your constitution, jumpstart your batteries, and help eliminate the negative psychological effects of the malaise. Some black teas, such as many of the Ceylon and Assam varieties, turn red in the cup when prepared. You might want to try a reddish-colored herbal infusion such as hibiscus, honeybush, rooibos, or rosehip.

Pink, which combines red and white, is a feminine color that invites feelings of nurturing love, warmth, and physical tranquility. I've seen artwork displayed on pink walls to striking effect. If you're a single woman desiring romance and partnership, feng shui experts say you should paint your bedroom pink to attract love.

Red's complementary color is green.

Orange

Like red, orange is a stimulating color. But the energy emitted by this combination of red and yellow is gentler and associated more with the warmth of sociability, abundance, joy, and comfort. Shades and tints of orange such as peach and salmon work well in dining rooms because these hues are said to quicken the appetite and foster congeniality. It seems that these days, orange has become a fad color for restaurants. Several eateries in my town sport bright orange signs, slick tangerine-colored chairs and tables, and salmon-colored walls. Some color psychologists claim that love of this color reveals a frivolous personality, yet orange is also said to foster the intellect because of its traditional association with the planet Mercury. According to feng shui, it's also the color of motherhood and marriage.

I once painted my bedroom a salmon color and found it cozy and relaxing. The warm and vibrant feeling of the room so impressed an artist friend that he painted his studio the same color. He said it showed his paintings to their best advantage, as it does for the lithographs I've hung on my walls.

In my opinion, orange pekoe tea—a fairly common kind of black tea—is one of the best to take to my sanctuary after a meal because it eases my digestion and energizes me. Another tea that appears either orange or red in the cup is Ceylon, which is said to improve cardiovascular function. If you're tired of drinking tea in your haven, try a mango lassi. It tastes fabulous on a hot afternoon and has the added benefit of helping you contemplate the power and purpose of your life.

Orange's complementary color is blue.

Yellow

Many people link yellow with the warmth of the sun, cheerfulness, and good health. In African myth this hue is said to drive away evil and resolve conflicts.

Since yellow is the most visible color in the spectrum, the eye focuses sharply on it. People who drive a lot for work understand that yellow-colored vehicles are the safest on the road. My father, whose job took him all over Michigan, invariably bought yellow or white cars. When my mother's eyesight was failing, she bought reams of yellow-colored paper to write her grocery lists, memos, and just about everything else so her writing would show up better.

Sunny yellow seems brighter than white but doesn't tire the eyes the way white can. Because this hue also makes a room look smaller, it's good for painting large, lofty spaces such as an art museum or the great room in your house. It also makes an appropriate choice for a windowless bathroom because the color imitates fresh, clean sunlight. Since one of yellow's complementary colors is purple, purple accents almost always look attractive in a yellow room.

Yellow encourages emotional strength and diplomacy in tough situations. Coupled with the cool intellect of blue, another of yellow's complementary colors, it makes a happy, refreshing choice for an inner sanctum. In the dining room, yellow's luminous glow fosters friendly conversation; cool blue accents tame stress.

To enhance these qualities in yourself, try meditating in your sanctuary over a cup of white tea. Many white teas look yellow when brewed. White teas detoxify the body and help prevent cancer better than other kinds. Dragonwell green tea also looks yellow in the cup. Sip it while contemplating how to overcome a bad habit, seek clarity in a situation, or gain self-confidence.

Green

Green is the quintessential color of balance as it stands midway in the color spectrum. Psychologically, an affinity for green, which mixes equal parts of blue and yellow, may indicate a desire to withdraw from the outside world. It may also show a need for rest, reassurance, peace, and harmony.

The spaces where actors await their turns on stage or television talk shows are universally known as "green rooms" because this hue is thought to calm preshow butterflies.

Science has shown that green lowers blood pressure, which makes this color ideal for concentration and reflection. Green encourages us to contemplate simple, bucolic scenes because it doesn't require the eye to focus. This makes it a relaxing choice for a bedroom or meditation space.

Recently I painted my computer room light green. I find it helps me concentrate by withdrawing from external stimuli and meditating on the subjects about which I'm writing. I accented the green by painting the molding black with a dark red stripe along the middle in an effort to lend an Asian flair. Green also makes the room look larger—a real bonus in my nineteenth-century home with its cramped spaces. On the downside, depending on the shade, this color can appear a bit bland and enervating.

Although many shades of green exist for decorating your sanctuary, this hue can be difficult to match. I suggest that when going forth on a decorating expedition, you carry your paint sample with you so you can coordinate better. Yellow-green is a soothing neutral color. Blue-green, like the sea, calms the nerves, eases muscle tension, and stimulates cardiovascular circulation.

No matter which kind of green you choose, or even if you don't select this hue for your walls, you can bring a bit of green energy into your sanctuary to balance body, mind, and spirit. For this I suggest matcha, a powdered green Japanese tea. Simply add hot water to it for drinking. Matcha tea helps strengthen bones and teeth and minimizes hair loss; at the same time, it relaxes the body. If you don't care for the taste in a tea, try eating green ice cream that uses matcha as a base. A peppier green tea comes from the peppermint herb, which is excellent for seeking a new beginning.

Green's complementary color is red.

Blue

It has long been thought that this cool, passive, and relaxing color embodies the subtle energy of the origin of life. Through time and many cultures, it's a favorite color both for clothing and living spaces. Blue is associated with spirituality. It symbolizes harmony, loyalty, inspiration, devotion, honesty, and serenity. It's suitable for your sanctuary because blue creates a mood conducive to meditation, spiritual awareness, self-discovery, guidance, patience, and understanding.

This color makes a space look cooler and somewhat bigger for its size, so it's not necessarily the best choice for large spaces. Blue also helps curb the appetite, so if you want to shed a few pounds, you might consider painting your dining space in this hue rather than using appetite-stimulating orange.

Like green, blue is a tricky color to match. My advice is to gather beforehand all the blue materials you want for your room, such as paint, wallpaper, drapery, linens, and pillows. This way, you don't have to hunt and peck through the stores or online for just the right items to match or complement each other. And while I'm on the subject of online shopping, this is one area where I believe you should visit the physical store rather than shop on your computer to get the best feel for textures and colors.

Blue rooms are ideal for rest and relaxation, but not for detailed work, reading, or intense study. This is because the eye doesn't focus blue light well.

Add a couple of drops of chamomile essence, which is blue, to white tea for relaxation and meditation in your sanctuary. To produce the same effect, blend your favorite smoothie and add a few blueberries to tint it blue. Blueberries are good for your health, too. They're packed with fiber, folate, potassium, and vitamins C and B6, which support heart health and good cholesterol. Blueberries are thought to discourage any negative vibes from seeping into your thoughts.

Orange is blue's complementary color.

Purple

This color is the last visible wavelength before the ultraviolet ray. Like blue, purple focuses light softly, so I don't recommend it for a room where you spend much of your time doing detailed work, typing on the computer, or reading. On the other hand, this hue has universal aesthetic appeal because it combines the earthiness of red with the spiritual qualities of blue. Purple also fosters creativity. I've noticed that artists seem to be drawn to the color purple. This hue is also an emblem of spiritual power and idealism.

Lighter shades such as violet tend to be tranquilizing and so are appropriate for bedrooms. Violet is a spiritual color, believed to take awareness to a high level to contemplate the mysteries of time, space, and the cosmos. This makes it a superb choice for a meditation space. My bathroom is done in violet for spirituality, blue for relaxation, and white for hygiene. I love soaking and meditating in the tub, although I admit I haven't floated off into the cosmos yet. Although purple's complementary color is yellow, white seemed appropriate for my bathroom because it encourages cleanliness.

Any concoction made with purple fruit will infuse you with the antioxidant anthocyanin, which will help protect your body from the free radicals that cause cancer. Since purple is a high-powered color, on a psychological level it can help strengthen your will, break a streak of persistent bad luck, and bring long-term plans to fruition. Concord grape juice is a fine example of a purple-colored fruit you can take to your sanctuary.

White

White is a balanced color because white light combines all the colors of the visible spectrum, which reflect back to the perceiver. In many cultures white symbolizes spirituality, purity, simplicity, and good hygiene. In some cultures it also stands for death.

I don't recommend all-white walls for your sanctuary because white's brightness causes the pupil of the eye to contract, which may distract your attention and even cause headaches. The stark, cold, sterile white walls of some sanitariums of former times have been known to drive emotionally distraught patients around the bend. Now that color psychology is better understood, hospitals and institutions tend to decorate in more cheerful hues of orange, yellow, rose, and light green.

If you want to use white in your inner sanctum, I suggest you combine it with other colors. My dining room walls are white to counterbalance the dark walnut trim and brown of the hardwood floor. The white also highlights my collectibles on the plate racks. Since white's opposite is black, you can create a chic, modern-looking space by combining these opposites.

If you've never tasted white tea, now's the time to experiment with imbibing it in your retreat. White tea can be drunk to enhance your meditation experience and help you contemplate your spiritual goals. This type of tea contains very little caffeine because the new leaves and buds used to make it are dried immediately after harvesting. This is also the reason white tea is full of antioxidants, especially vitamin C. The polyphenols in it can help minimize wrinkles, especially when used in a face cream. The taste is quite mild, not at all grassy like some green teas. Silver Needles and White Peony are popular choices.

Brown

In general, brown is the color of earth and wood, a combination of red, yellow, and black. It's considered a receptive and grounding color, linked to strength, stability, serenity, security, and the natural rhythms of life. Brown encourages a person to slow down and relax. It's masculine and weighty in nature but not as harsh as black. This hue encourages deep concentration. However, on its own, it can appear a bit stodgy and humorless. When combined with other colors, brown works well in a personal retreat. Choose neutral tones such as cream or coffee, or even sage, light green, orange-yellow, or aqua as balancers.

If you're a coffee lover, you'll be ecstatic to know that coffee makes as fine a brew as tea to drink in your sanctuary. There are also as many shades of coffee as shades of brown, depending on how it's brewed. You get all the virtues of brown in a cup of coffee as well as improved alertness and focus. This drink also helps ward off diabetes because it contains a fair amount of chromium and magnesium, which help the body use insulin. If, like me, you're not a coffee drinker, you can always munch on a bowlful of figs or drink hot cocoa to experience the virtues of brown.

Gray

I remember the color gray as a favorite of corporate offices during the 1980s. Practically every business I walked into was decorated with shades of gray and off-white, alleviated by occasional burgundy highlights. You may love gray; if you do, I encourage you to go for it as the dominant color for your space. In color psychology it is said that using a lot of gray in decor reveals anxiety or lack of confidence, yet it can look sharp combined with black, turquoise, shades of orange, and some neutral tones. In feng shui this color is said to attract helpful people to your life and encourage experiences outside the home such as travel and international trade.

Black

Black has become one of the "in" colors for home and office decor as it is considered bold and powerful. Black makes a statement that promises glamor and sophistication.

Black and white, its opposite, look elegant when combined in room decor.

This hue is beneficial in meditations that require deep concentration—for example, for psychic work. I have used this color effectively when I needed to draw forth a miracle from a deeply hidden, almost impossible situation. For this, I used black candles and meditation cloth. It can also create a positive environment for success in business, especially when a black object is placed in the north. Be aware that too much black in your space can be weakening and depressing. Here's an example.

A friend from my women's spirituality group decided to convert her spare bedroom into a meditation space. Since she had trouble staying focused, she thought it would help to paint the room completely black, including the ceiling and floor.

The first time I visited, I was overcome with a wave of sadness, as if I'd gone into mourning, and I felt claustrophobic almost to the point of choking. Believe me, this was a very uncomfortable, almost menacing sensation. I was reminded of the gloomy Rolling Stones song "Paint It Black."

My friend soon became equally dissatisfied with the room's decoration. She set about lightening the ambiance with wallpaper of a purple, violet, and yellow design. She also sanded away the paint from the floor and stained it brown. Then she added splashes of color, including white, magenta, and violet-colored meditation pillows. Finally, she placed along a sunny window ledge pots brimming with forced paperwhite narcissus, daffodil, and hyacinth bulbs that looked cheerful and exuded a heavenly fragrance.

I can't think of a kind of black tea to take to your haven. But you can always carry in a bowlful of black olives along with a hunk of contrasting white feta or goat cheese to satisfy the munchies.

No matter what combination of colors you choose for your sanctuary, you can enhance or mute them depending on the kind of light you use. Dim light makes colors appear more vivid, and bright light moderates them. Colored lights dazzle the eyes and make a dramatic impression, while colored surfaces don't affect the vision as intensely. This means you may be more deeply moved if, for example, you were to shine a blue light on your meditation focal point as opposed to placing it in a blue room.

Color Psychology

Because of the resurgence of interest in the psychological effects of color, investigators are reevaluating the art and science of color psychology. Nowadays, these associated topics elicit plenty of contradictory opinions about the best colors to use for the home. If you Google this year's and last year's decorating trends, you'll see little consensus about home decor. Such lack of agreement is rivaled only by that of the capricious fashion industry.

Part of the reason for these disagreements is that, like reactions to scent, people's reactions to color can be very individual. No matter how a person responds to different hues, one thing is certain: the influence of color on our daily lives is pervasive. We seethe green with envy, see red when we're angry, have tangerine dreams, sink into blue funks, say we're in the pink when all is going well, and some of us even pen purple prose!

Advertisers understand that color can influence our opinions and use its allure to sell us products. Who hasn't seen a TV advertisement about that little purple pill or a commercial showing a close-up of crisp golden waffles surrounded by mounds of snowy whipped cream and ripe red strawberries? Then there's the toilet paper with pictures of fluffy white clouds on the package. And how about that gigantic pea-green-colored fellow hawking vegetables in a verdant field?

What Color Can Say About You

The colors you select for your sanctuary can reveal a lot about your personality and psyche. Experiments show that most people are oriented primarily toward either warm or cold colors. Take a look at the dominant colors of clothing in your closet to see which end of the spectrum attracts you most. If warm colors like red, orange, pink, and yellow appeal, then you probably are a physically active type who enjoys social action and expresses your feelings openly. You are generally open and receptive to outside influences. On the downside, you may feel uncomfortable in an environment where you're left on your own and need to make decisions with no external input.

If you enjoy solitary pursuits and are inwardly directed, your closet is probably full of clothing in the cool shades of green, blue, purple, brown, gray, and black. You're undoubtedly a deep thinker who doesn't want to make mistakes, so you contemplate every move from all angles before you act. You may also be shy in social situations and shrink from crowds. Because of this orientation, some people may wrongly think you are unemotional and lack sympathy for others.

Where you live geographically also seems to affect color preferences. It's been theorized that because the human eye filters light differently according to our physical location in respect to the equator, this filtering process accounts for differing color choices. People living in cooler northern climes tend to select blue, while those dwelling in tropical or semitropical regions generally prefer red. On the other hand, when I lived in Brazil, I noticed most homes I visited had gray or eggshell colored walls, which blows this color theory out of the water. Then again, my personal experience is anecdotal at best.

Experiments in color psychology have revealed that although color preferences cut across racial lines, gender appears to make a difference. For example, women normally select yellow over orange, while men choose orange over yellow. Popularly, it is claimed that athletes like energetic red, intellectuals are drawn to contemplative blue, the convivial are attracted to chatty orange, and artists prefer shades of purple. Of course, individual favorites can vary widely. In the end, your personal color preferences are what's most important to you when you embark on your decorating adventure. If you're happy with the result, this is all that matters.

Synesthesia

Some people, especially the creative, enjoy a special affinity to color. The sound of a certain musical note may cause you to taste the flavor of root beer. Or, when you feel a cool, misty breeze, you can hear the soft sound of seagulls flapping their wings in the distance. In this condition, known as synesthesia, stimulation of one of the senses kindles another. Some synesthetics, as these people are called, see colors when they experience certain smells, tastes, alphabet letters, and sounds. American rapper, singer, and songwriter Pharrell Williams is a synesthetic whose composition "Happy" sings to him in shades of yellow with mustard and orange sherbet accents. Kanye and Lady Gaga have reported similar sensations.

To some extent, we all possess this faculty. The scores of adjectives we use to describe various teas, coffees, and wines provide examples. Famous wine expert Jamie Smith (voted America's Best Sommelier by *Food and Wine* magazine) speaks of the Nebbiolo grape in terms of smell and color. When he sniffs this grape, he says it smells like a purple and brown braided knot. As he continues sniffing, the knot slowly unwinds to bloom red. If you find the notion of synesthesia fascinating, you might try developing this gift when meditating in your sanctuary. A sharpened sense of synesthesia can add a new dimension to your enjoyment of life.

The Taste of Color

While we're on the subject of smelling and tasting color, here's a Brazilian recipe for a smoothie that may help you to taste, smell, or see the color green because its primary ingredient is avocado. The purpose of introducing this delightful drink is to get you to think more deeply about this hue. And it doesn't hurt that this smoothie is loaded with vitamins; in fact, Brazilians call this category of drinks "vitaminas." And, oh yes, this drink tastes heavenly, too! After you prepare the beverage, take it to your personal space. Contemplate the rich green color for a while, and then slowly sip, letting the concept of greenness percolate through your body.

AVOCADO SMOOTHIE

1 cup whole milk
1 avocado, peeled, pitted, and chopped
½ cup old-fashioned oatmeal
¼ teaspoon cinnamon
3–4 ice cubes

You can add some honey as a sweetener (in my opinion, if the avocado is fresh, it's sweet enough on its own). Place everything in a blender and process until smooth.

Healing with Color

In this last segment on color, I'd like to turn the discussion to using color in your sanctuary for healing. Healing with color is performed in the science of chromotherapy. Chromotherapists, as these healers are called, use color to cure ailments because they believe that disease is rooted in an imbalance at one or more levels of the physical and spiritual bodies. To restore harmony, chromotherapists sometimes beam colored lights that vibrate at different rates on the afflicted areas or prescribe a diet rich in certain colors.

You don't have to saturate your private space with a specific color to accomplish a healing. The appropriate colored candle or cloth on the surface of your focal point and perhaps a suitable oil to anoint the candle and/or incense will work very well. Use color either to attract an influence toward you or send it in an outward direction, depending on whether you use a particular color or its complementary hue. You can do the following color healing meditation for yourself or someone else (with their permission).

For the purpose of this exercise, I use a system with a slightly different color scale than the one for home decoration. Instead of calling the colors "opposite" or "complementary," they are termed "positive" and "negative." The positive color's energy flows outward and away from you, and the negative energy flows toward you. In this case "negative" does not mean bad, just opposite; it is a void needing to be filled. The negative color attracts a certain force to you and the positive color flows outward to help heal another person, animal, or situation.

This system is based on certain theories about the seven traditional planets of our solar system. Here are short synopses for the impact of each traditional planet on health, along with their corresponding positive and negative colors:

Saturn

POSITIVE COLOR: indigo

NEGATIVE COLOR: black

HEALTH CONCERNS: acute illness, geriatrics, the skeletal system, stopping the progress of a disease, hair, bones, death

Jupiter

POSITIVE COLOR: purple

NEGATIVE COLOR: blue

HEALTH CONCERNS: improving ill physical health, spiritual health, adrenal glands, arteries, liver, pancreas

Mars

POSITIVE COLOR: red

NEGATIVE COLOR: red

HEALTH CONCERNS: surgery, energy level, personal magnetism, heart, blood, muscular system, motor nerves, physical wounds

Sun

POSITIVE COLOR: orange

NEGATIVE COLOR: yellow or gold

HEALTH CONCERNS: vitality, mental health, spine, physical health, heart, thyroid, pituitary, spleen

Venus

POSITIVE COLOR: emerald green

NEGATIVE COLOR: emerald green

HEALTH CONCERNS: the emotions, youthfulness, cheeks, chin, kidneys, hair, skin, throat, thyroid, testicles, sense of touch, veins

Mercury

POSITIVE COLOR: yellow

NEGATIVE COLOR: orange

HEALTH CONCERNS: general health, mouth, nervous system, bowels, throat, vocal cords, pulmonary and respiratory circulation, brain, thyroid, parathyroid. When in doubt about which planet to choose, Mercury is a safe bet because it is known as the "planetary physician."

Moon

POSITIVE COLOR: blue

NEGATIVE COLOR: puce (brownish purple)

HEALTH CONCERNS: psychic health, mental health and stability, uterus, ovaries, medulla, lymphatic system, nervous system, breasts, esophagus, pituitary and thyroid

When you meditate on a specific planet's negative energy (for example, orange in the following exercise), visualize that this hue surrounds and saturates both you and your environment, drawing the color's energy to you and making you receptive to reaping its benefits. When you meditate on the planet's positive color (yellow or gold in the exercise that follows), you are gathering up all the energy associated with the color and sending it toward someone or something else.

Sun Healing Meditation in Orange

Let's say you're recovering from a long illness and could use an extra infusion of solar energy to help you feel tiptop or at least like your old self. If you have an orange cloth, lay it on top of a flat surface such as a dresser, coffee table, or anywhere you can sit comfortably to meditate undisturbed for ten minutes. Rub an orange candle with neroli oil. Secure it in a candleholder and set it on top of the cloth. Next, take an incense burner and position it next to the candle. Light a quick-burning coal in the burner and sprinkle a few grains of frankincense resin, also known as church incense, on the hot coal.

Light the candle and take a seat in front of the table. While watching the candle flame, meditate for a few minutes on the illness from which you are recovering, reviewing in your mind all of its stages until you come to the symptoms you're still experiencing. Now, mentally put aside all of those thoughts. If necessary, visualize the symptoms, side effects, and lingering weaknesses being carried away with the smoke from the incense and being dispelled in the air. Or imagine you are stuffing all the bad, negative, and wrong into a steel box and burying it deep in the ground, where the earth will neutralize it. Next, visualize yourself being surrounded by a joyful orange healing light that infuses your body. See yourself completely cured from what ails you.

Inhale the sweet aroma of the incense, exhale completely, then gaze again into the depths of the candle flame. Repeat aloud the following affirmation:

> *As life is miraculously revitalized by the energy emanating from the sun, which even in its darkest hour returns to light the earth, may I, too, be strengthened by its healing light. In my state of pure receptivity, I feel solar warmth flowing into my being like a gentle spring breeze. I am healed and whole again, brimming with energy, ready to experience the joys and challenges of life again with renewed strength and vitality.*

Continue gazing at the candle flame for a few minutes. Don't worry if you don't feel immediately energized. Just remain open and receptive to the sun's healing rays. After a few minutes, take a deep breath, exhale, and extinguish the candle flame and the incense. Within the next few days, your health is bound to rally.

You can direct this healing toward another person by using a yellow or gold cloth, candle, frankincense incense, and heliotrope oil. Place a photo of the person on the table and direct the solar energy toward that individual. Get the person's permission to do this healing, as it is not nice to do anything to anybody without their knowledge. Tell the recipient when you're going to perform the meditation so they can mentally attend the session.

three

Feng Shui Made Easy

Now that you've had time to put down the paint can and brush and revel in your newly colored space, it's time to explore other ways to activate and personalize your sanctuary. Here I'll demystify some concepts surrounding the venerable Chinese tradition of feng shui.

Feng shui (pronounced "fung shway") is a system for establishing harmony in your environment. In recent years this ancient Chinese art has been trending in the West, and many people aspire to add a bit of feng shui magic to their homes and lives. Who can blame them? After all, practitioners claim that applying its principles to your immediate surroundings will help you reap the benefits of a happy, healthy, wealthy life, and most of us want that. Nevertheless, enthusiasts often stop short when they realize how intricate the application of feng shui can get. Their hectic schedules and complicated lives don't allow them enough time and patience to immerse themselves into an in-depth study of this subtle art. This is where I may be able to help.

In this chapter I present a general overview of the basic principles of this art and offer some practical suggestions on how to make feng shui bring positive energy and balance to your home without having to delve too deeply into the details. If what I say stimulates you to learn more, I recommend checking online, at a bookstore, or the library for some of the many informative books dedicated exclusively to the subject. The resources section at the end of this book also offers suggestions. If you don't have the time to read up on the topic and want quick action, you can always hire a feng shui master. Yes, these experts in the field really do exist. Most of them have studied this system for years and are quite familiar with the ins and outs of what they term as "the art of placement" and its symbolism.

Feng shui originated in China over three thousand years ago as an outgrowth of the philosophy of life called Taoism. In many respects, it advocates a return to a simpler, more intuitive way of living. In short, it is a way to enrich your living and working spaces by attuning them to the laws of nature.

In Taoism it is believed that everything in the universe springs from two opposing forces known as yin and yang. Yin is roughly equivalent to the Western concept of the moon. Its qualities are feminine, receptive, absorbing, soft, curved, cool, dark, fluid, and decreasing. Yin embodies earth, water, night, death, and rest. Yang, on the other hand, is like the Western conception of the sun. Its force is masculine, energetic, giving, hard, angular, fiery, bright, aggressive, and increasing. Yang represents the heavens, fire, daylight, life, and activity.

Taoism teaches that we should strive for harmony and balance of the yin and yang forces as well as an understanding of our connection to nature. Feng shui masters apply certain laws of nature to the home. Nature is represented by the five basic elements: fire, water, earth, metal, and wood. Taoists believe that the interaction of these elements creates order and structure in the world. In feng shui it is thought that you can use representations of the elements in your home to balance yin/yang energies and forge a harmonious environment. The elements combine to create a strong and powerful connection as follows: fire assists earth, earth assists metal, metal assists water, water assists wood, and wood assists fire. This positive result then passes on to you.

Yet as much as the elements can generate constructively, they can also damage and destroy. In fact, an overbalance of any one element can be ravaging. Take water, for example. Without it, all life would perish. A warm shower on a cold winter's evening or a cool drink after a day in the hot sun can be restorative, but a tsunami can wipe out an entire city. Everything needs to be in balance in order to thrive. In that vein, fire melts metal, metal cuts wood, wood moves earth, earth dams water, and water puts out fire. In feng shui the kind of objects you place in your environment and where you put them can either encourage an underbalanced element to flourish or diminish an overbalance of the element.

Another important principle of feng shui has to do with the belief that a life force called *chi* (pronounced "chee") flows through all objects and nature in general. Chi is the term used to describe the essential energy of life and its movement. It is believed that when chi flows smoothly in an undulating pattern, it is moving in harmony with the laws of nature. When you embrace chi, you are going with the flow, so to speak.

On the other hand, if you allow the chi in your environment to stagnate, linger, rush by, or provoke, you incur *sha* (literally, "an obnoxious vapor"). This negative energy can generate misfortune on any or all fronts.

How to Apply Feng Shui in Your Home

When feng shui practitioners inspect a home for energy flow, they divide it into eight corners, using the eight points of the compass as a basis for laying out space. In this brief overview, you need only consider the most important position, which is called the center. This spot represents you.

Go to the center of your house, apartment, sanctuary, studio, office, or garden. Feng shui also relies on intuition, so if you live in a house with more than one story, let your intuition guide you as to which floor contains the center. The element is earth, the colors are yellow and earth tones, and the shape is square or rectangular. The chi from all the other areas converges and culminates in the center, which is why it is the most powerful area of the house. The center is a fitting spot to place a focal point for contemplation and spiritual development.

Since this area is associated with the earth, it is where you should feel the most grounded. To keep chi flowing freely around the center, display reminders of the earth element here. Choose items like earthenware vessels or rock, mineral, and crystal specimens. Square shapes, like a square or rectangular focal point, and yellow or earth-toned objects are also appropriate.

You can stop here with your venture into the mysteries of feng shui, skip to the tips section, and still reap many benefits. However, if you want to dig a little deeper, read on.

To continue, you will need a compass.

Now, with compass in hand, imagine that your central point marks the center of a wheel. Stand there facing south. Pivot to your right one-eighth of the way around your imaginary wheel. This direction is southwest. Another eighth of the way is west, then northwest, north, northeast, and so on until you have made it 360 degrees around the entire wheel. Each direction, also known as a corner, denotes a specific type of influence on your life where you want to keep the positive chi flowing and defray destructive sha.

Following is a list of the corners, the type of chi they embody, their influences, element associations, colors, shapes, the type of sha you need to be wary of, and appropriate furniture and objects to place in the corner. Don't feel you need to clutter all the corners with things. After all, feng shui is also a way to simplify your life. A single, small representation of even one of the suggested objects in a corner where you feel you really need help to get the chi flowing will do nicely. As your needs change, so can the objects you put there.

South

CHI: vigorous

INFLUENCES: joy, opportunities, fame, respect, reputation, longevity

ELEMENTS: fire, wood

COLORS: red, green

SHAPES: triangular material such as throw rugs decorated with geometrical shapes

FURNITURE: fireplace, stove heater, anything made from animal products such as leather, silk, bone, or wool

OBJECTS: pyramid, cone, candles, lamps, aroma diffusers, feathers, soft-leafed plants

SHA: accelerating (think of your foot getting stuck on your vehicle's accelerator and you'll understand how frightening and exhausting accelerating sha can feel as it speeds by)

The main entrance or entrance to your sanctuary is considered to be located in this corner, even if the direction isn't really south. While all areas of the home should be kept clean and clutter-free, it is especially important to keep the main entrance unobstructed so the chi flows smoothly.

Southwest

CHI: soothing

INFLUENCES: peace, happiness, romance, purity, motherhood, partnership

ELEMENTS: earth, fire

COLORS: pink, peach, yellow, red, cream, white (avoid green)

SHAPES: flat, square
FURNITURE: made from any material except wood
OBJECTS: pictures of loved ones and families,
pictures of yourself with others, pink candles,
bowls, statues, hearts, anything that brings you
joy
SHA: disruptive, tending to cause irrational behavior

While feng shui masters recommend you always display pairs of objects instead of single ones, it is especially important in this corner, which represents love, friendship, and marriage. For example, hanging a picture of you by yourself could cause feelings of loneliness and emptiness.

West

CHI: calming
INFLUENCES: pleasure, creativity, socializing,
entertainment, children
ELEMENTS: metal, earth
COLORS: cream, pastel, white
SHAPES: circles, ovals
FURNITURE: entertainment center, metal furniture,
easel
OBJECTS: computer, your journal, sewing/
mending things, tools, small kitchen appliances,
gemstones, your or your family's artwork, games
SHA: dangerous, tending to cause rash behavior

Since this corner fosters creativity, it's a great place to let the whimsical side of your nature reveal itself in your decoration. Don't decorate with red here, especially red flowers.

Northwest

CHI: expansive

INFLUENCES: communications, travel, outside
interests, fatherhood, helpful people, fresh starts

ELEMENTS: metal, earth

COLORS: gray, black

SHAPES: arches, circles

FURNITURE: desk, computer

OBJECTS: current contracts, materials relating
to current projects, seedlings (if the light is
strong enough),world map, globe, travel poster,
souvenirs collected from past trips, picture of a
mentor or another person you admire or an angel

SHA: unpredictable, leading to unsettling feelings

This corner represents communications central for your
home. Place your landline here or charge your cell phone in
this area. Store business cards and addresses in this quad-
rant. It is also your wishing corner, where you can display a
symbol of something you ardently desire.

North

CHI: nurturing

INFLUENCES: career, life's journey, business success,
personal growth, musical and artistic talent

ELEMENTS: water, metal

COLORS: deep purple, navy, black

SHAPES: wavy, undulating

FURNITURE: glass furniture such as a table with a
glass top; tapestry blanket or upholstery with a
wavy print

OBJECTS: shells, tabletop fountain, aquarium, waterfall, anything with a reflective surface such as a mirror, pictures of seascapes or sailboats or fish

SHA: unpredictable, leading to unsettling feelings

If you're feeling stuck in your career, obtain a photo of a successful person in your field from a magazine, newspaper, or online search, and mount it on the wall.

Northeast
CHI: flourishing

INFLUENCES: knowledge, academic success, spiritual growth, wisdom, meditation

ELEMENTS: earth, fire

COLORS: yellow, tan, turquoise

SHAPES: square, low, flat

FURNITURE: bookcase, instruction manuals, focal point or altar

OBJECTS: books; photo of a mentor; pictures of mountains or desert; tranquil, earthy scenes; no live plants or trees here

SHA: stagnating, leading to illness

This area makes a good place to study.

East
CHI: stimulating

INFLUENCES: family, health, nutrition, rebirth

ELEMENTS: wood, water

COLORS: green, aqua, blue

SHAPES: tall, narrow, cylindrical

FURNITURE: wood furniture, exercise equipment, floral print upholstery

OBJECTS: family heirlooms, pictures of gardens, flowers, landscapes, plant on a pedestal, tall vase, storage area for health herbs, a treasure from childhood

SHA: stagnating, leading to illness

If the energy flow is obstructed here, the overpowering sha can make you feel egotistical and vain.

Southeast

CHI: protective

INFLUENCES: prosperity, abundance, material world

ELEMENTS: wood, water

COLORS: purple, green

SHAPES: columnar, cylindrical

FURNITURE: antique furniture from the family

OBJECTS: your valued collections, three coins, mirror, crystals, piggy bank, aquarium

SHA: provocative, causing headaches and irritability

Chinese restaurants often place their cash registers here.

Quick Tips to Eliminate Sha and Get Chi to Flow

No space is perfect. Your sanctuary may face a long, straight hall or a street that encourages the chi to rush through too quickly. Your home may be located near a graveyard, or perhaps you have unfriendly neighbors. Exposed rafters may divide a room; the toilet or your bed may face the door. Perhaps you live in an apartment and rules prohibit you from repainting the walls a more compatible color. Never fear! For every feng shui problem, a remedy exists. Here are some tips on converting harmful sha into beneficial chi. In many ways, they correspond to what you've already read about stimulating the five senses in your haven.

Sound

Bells, music, flowing water, and wind chimes can all help to deflect provoking sha emanating from the southeast and invite chi to flow peacefully. A good corner to install the sound system for your entire home is in the west, the entertainment corner. Remember to use sound judiciously in other areas of your home as well. However, avoid hanging bells in the east or southeast; these corners are governed by wood, which metal destroys.

Stillness

The feeling of calm and quiet can be used in feng shui to repel overpowering sha proceeding from the east. Items that suggest tranquility might include an elegant vase, a sparkling gemstone, a well-executed picture of a pastoral scene, or even a statue of a serene, smiling Buddha. Always put statues on a pedestal, never on the ground.

Light

Although all corners of the home should be well-lit, light is especially indicated in the south to dispel accelerating sha and activate positive chi. Mirrors can also turn away negativity. If you place a mirror facing your front door, any kind of sha that dares try to enter will be deflected. Make sure your mirror is all in one piece and not divided, though, or your luck may also get divided and scamper away.

Color

Harmonious pastel shades disperse disruptive sha, especially when it emanates from the southwest. Overly bright colors, on the other hand, may activate stagnating sha. If you can't or don't want to paint an entire room in pastels, add a throw pillow, blanket, rug, or picture that displays the soothing colors.

Movement

Feng shui's goal is to enable chi to flow unobstructed and for sha to dissipate from all areas of your space. Decorations that mimic gently flowing motion are one way to achieve this aim. Tabletop fountains or waterfalls, a piece of furniture with curled carvings, incense smoke, wind chimes, flags fluttering in the breeze from an open window, mobiles, items decorated with scintillating sequins—even a television—will convince lingering sha to skedaddle and invite invigorating chi to flow.

Straight Lines

According to feng shui philosophy, only very short, straight lines exist in nature. Long, straight lines such as corridors and highways run contrary to the natural harmony of things. Yet under some circumstances, especially when dangerous sha is detected, straight lines can sidetrack this negative energy away from your environment. Use anything that forms a straight line, like the edge of a piece of furniture or a fan, flute, scroll, stick, or oar to deflect the negative energy.

Life

Adding a bit of life to your haven can go a long way toward dissipating lingering sha, especially in the north, and instilling your space with vitality. If you feel the energy in any area is wilting, install an aquarium stocked with live fish or get a bird in a cage. Soft, round-leafed plants also make a good choice. Succulents are okay, but not cacti because their spikes draw dangerous sha. If you have a dog or cat—and depending on the room and convenience—you can also place the pet's bed in this area. Just don't pair a bird in a cage with the cat's pillow!

Fragrance

Fragrance is a splendid way to harmonize your environment. You can use fresh flowers, aroma diffusers, incense, potpourri, or air fresheners. See chapter 5 for specific fragrance ideas. If you are allergic to scent or have another medical reason to avoid it, simply open a window in good weather and let the natural aromas of nature envelop you.

Devices

Unpredictable sha emanating from the northwest can be tamed with tools and equipment such as electrical appliances, computers, television sets, shop tools, and kitchen gadgets. Even a wall calendar or calculator will do the trick. Heavy objects like statues and pedestals will also banish sha.

Here are some additional tips:

- Crystals disperse negative energy. Hang one in a dark corner to stimulate chi.
- Keep the toilet seat down and the door to the bathroom closed (unless you keep your kitty's litter there).
- Place statues of dogs or lions on either side of your front door for protection.
- Fix dripping faucets or your luck might flush down the drain and engender a big water bill.
- Decorate with pairs of knickknacks, as singletons are considered unlucky.
- Avoid using too much black; this hue can drain away chi, especially in the bedroom. One exception is in the north to actuate success in business. Also keep a black rug at the front entrance to attract wealth and luck.
- Don't bring dried flowers into your hallowed space, as they can instigate trouble in your love life (not to mention that they attract cobwebs and dust). You don't need to always use fresh flowers; plastic or silk work fine. If you prefer and can afford fresh flowers, discard wilting blossoms; they are so sad! Chrysanthemums are a good choice for most corners of your home, as they represent long life, a long and successful career, and a long and happy marriage.
- I know cacti are trending because they require little care, and I do mention them in a later

chapter. However, feng shui masters warn *not* to have them in the home because the sharp, spiky leaves act like poison arrows for the occupants. Substitute jade plants, which also require little care; they will draw wealth and good health.

- Declutter every part of the house, including inside the refrigerator (my *bête noir*), closet, and shelves, and clean these areas thoroughly. Above all, keep your front entrance clutter-free.

- Throw away faded, frayed linens and furniture coverings. Repair or discard broken things, and replace burned-out light bulbs right away.

- Place colorful artwork and mirrors in hallways to deflect the sha that these straight lines engender.

- Use an octagonal mirror to repel sha from your living space. Such common annoyances include overhead electrical lines, nearby dumpsters, trash bins, barking dogs, and outdoor lights from neighbors' houses or the street. For obvious reasons, never place a mirror in a position where it will cut off part of the reflection of your head.

- Don't place your bed so your feet face the bedroom door. This is known as the "killing" or "coffin" position because when someone dies at home, they are carried out feet first.

- Never locate a desk where you will need to sit with your back to the door or window. That way, nobody can stab you in the back physically or figuratively. The best dimensions for a desk are 35″ x 60″ x 33″.

A Relaxing and Balancing Tea

⌒〜⌒

Once you have arranged your space the way you like it, settle in and enjoy the positive, energizing, relaxing flow of chi as it circulates freely around you. Here is an herbal tea recipe to help you unwind and balance your chi at the same time.

½ teaspoon lavender flowers (fresh or dried)
¼ teaspoon chamomile flowers (fresh or dried)
Pink rose petals (fresh or dried)

Mix the botanicals together in a small bowl and place in a tea strainer. Prepare a cup of hot water (spring water is preferable though not necessary). Bring the water to a boil in a small pot (do not microwave, though, as the water heats unevenly in a microwave), and let it cool for 2 minutes. Now pour the water over the strainer full of botanicals and into the cup. Sweeten your tea with honey, if desired. As you sip, gaze around the home you have transformed into the perfect sanctuary and give yourself a pat on the back.

four

Your Sanctuary's Core

In this chapter we'll probe more deeply into how to use your sanctuary space for relaxation, meditation, and self-realization by creating a focal point. To do this, we'll concentrate on the core of your sacred space, the place where you bring everything together to honor, pray, or meditate. This location represents the heart of your sanctuary. It's where you feel free to unburden your troubles and anxieties, work on your shortcomings and goals, express your hopes and dreams, and communicate with the All-One, angels, deities, and spirits of other worlds—or simply retreat from the outside world and embrace solitude so you can relax and renew. Here you can be yourself without concerns over outside interference.

This spiritual focal point is often called an altar. The faithful of most religions worship at altars, whether in magnificent cathedrals, synagogues, mosques, temples, and churches, in humbler neighborhood houses of worship, or at devotional niches in the home. If you're not religious but still wish to explore your spiritual nature, consider this spot as a place of honor where all the positive energy you've mustered in the rest of your home can converge.

Your Bedroom

Before you start constructing your altar, you need to decide where to place it, which means you first want to establish your sanctuary's location. You can make a retreat anywhere; for me, it's my bedroom. This seems to me to be the most logical and natural place to commune with the life force and creative energy that flows through the universe. My bedroom is my safe haven and hearth that warms my entire home. Here I find rest, peace, and solitude but also intimacy. In this ultimate private space, I can let my guard down, dress any way I like, and do whatever I want. It's also where I hide out when I feel ill so I can recover.

Whether or not you choose your bedroom as your sanctuary, it's still a uniquely personal space that reflects your life and reveals what is harmonious or out of balance in your current situation. Therefore, it is the one room in your home that requires the most attention, especially if you're preparing it to be a sacred space.

Begin planning the room by taking a clear, unvarnished look at it. Is everything neat and tidy and in its proper place? No unmade bed, discarded pizza boxes, empty coffee cups lying about, magazines scattered around the floor, cobwebs on the ceiling, or dirt behind the door? Congratulations! You can move on to constructing your altar. However, if your bedroom could use a bit of sprucing up, you might contemplate what this says about harmony in your life.

The first step toward building an altar in your bedroom is to eliminate the clutter and give the room a thorough scrubbing. Even if you're Mary Poppins orderly, I recommend you purify and consecrate the room with the four elements at each of the four seasons of the year. For air, walk the perimeter with incense or a smudge stick; carry a lighted candle around all four corners for fire. For water, I suggest lightly spraying the walls with water from a bottle mister. Sprinkle salt for earth.

If you're having trouble getting started on this daunting task, you're in good company. Anne Gibbons, American cartoonist and illustrator, expressed this sentiment for all of us who are less-than-perfect housekeepers: "Nature abhors a vacuum, and so do I." Here's a tea recipe to help instill you with the courage to tackle this project.

"Shape Up the Ship" Tea

½ teaspoon loose gunpowder green tea or teabag
¼ teaspoon dried peppermint leaf
⅛ teaspoon dried parsley
2 pinches dried rosemary

Infuse the brew for 3 minutes in hot water. Drink up and get moving!

Once the space is clutter-free and trim as a Zen garden, take a deeper critical look. Note the type of lighting, both natural and artificial. Make sure it's reasonably bright but not harsh. Even if you live in an apartment and the landlord won't let you install track lights, you can purchase a couple of inexpensive small table lamps and bask in their cheery radiance.

Perhaps this room could use a fresh coat of paint or wallpaper. If your circumstances allow you to modify the walls, you may want to choose colors that are significant to you and that show your room to its best advantage. In feng shui the only colors frowned upon for a bedroom are too much red or yellow. This is because they are masculine yang colors that emit a lot of aggressive energy, which might keep you from getting enough sleep. After handling the visuals, go for sound, texture, smell, and even taste. If they're practical and fall within your budget, choose any elements that strike your fancy. Refer back to chapter 2 for ideas.

Don't Do These Things

Here's a short list of additional feng shui no-nos for the bedroom. You have every right to ignore the gurus' recommendations; what you choose to include or exclude from your sanctuary is your personal choice.

- Remove electrical equipment like computers, televisions, DVD players, and your cellphone, as the electromagnetic energy is harmful to health, rest, and fertility. (Personally, I find this suggestion impossible to follow. I love my little television set and confess I sometimes use the laptop in bed.)

- Besides not placing the bed so your feet face the door (the "coffin" position), don't put the head of the bed against a window or at a wall where a bathroom is located on the other side, as one's head must be protected at all times.
- Although keeping plants in your bedroom instills it with life, spiky plants such as cacti or sword plants are discouraged in bedrooms because it is believed that the forceful yang energy emitted by sharp foliage can disrupt rest.
- Don't put water features like tabletop fountains or aquariums here because their energy is too restless for this area. (My neighbor once installed an outdoor water fountain that ran constantly right next to my bedroom window. At first I thought I had an overflowing toilet. The most I could do to eliminate the sound was keep my windows on that side firmly shut. I was relieved when she had to remove the fountain after she bought a puppy.)

BENEFICIAL DREAM OIL

To facilitate dreams that may be helpful to you, such as those that help you solve a problem in your sleep, here's a little fragrance formula.

In a one-dram vial, place equal parts of frankincense, myrrh, and lily oils. Shake to blend. Before retiring, dab a drop on your third eye, the space between your brows.

BENEFICIAL DREAM TEA

Double your chances of success by also drinking a cup of beneficial dream tea before going to sleep.

½ teaspoon White Peony tea
¼ teaspoon kava kava
¼ teaspoon peppermint
A pinch of vervain

Place in a tea strainer. Put the strainer in a teacup and pour hot water over it. Let steep for 3 minutes before drinking. Sweet dreams!

Decorating Your Focal Point

Now find a secluded place for your altar within your sanctuary. Feng shui masters recommend positioning the altar across from the door or in the northwest. This corner symbolizes the father, who, by tradition, is the head of the household both spiritually and physically. Frankly, I don't see why you shouldn't also place it in the southwest corner to represent the mother, who is nurturing and also can be the head of the household. If another location in the room speaks to you, like a window, a shelf, or a bedside table, I recommend you go for it. If you live in a situation in which a permanent bedroom altar is inconvenient, refer to the discussion of portable altars later in this chapter for some ideas.

Since spaces are sanctified by intent, your motives will define your altar's design and purpose. Your altar may hold emblems of your cultural heritage, items that express your personality, and your most significant private symbols and mementos that speak directly to your soul. The objects on your altar should also help you concentrate your five senses to make your meditations as effective as possible. Make the arrangements eye-pleasing but not too busy. You can always change them around. Above all, don't confuse your altar with your overall sacrosanct space. Remember: the altar is the central focal point within this hallowed space. If the entire room or house were an altar, your energies might scatter and fade away.

The subconscious mind responds better to symbols than words, so the objects you select should engage the senses and symbolize concepts, wishes, or dreams you want to foster. Choose visually stimulating items to attract and keep your attention. A vase of fresh flowers will provide a splash of color and quicken your sense of smell. For sound, play soft music in the background or hang chimes that will catch the light breezes from an open window. A mixture of pleasing textures, such as a velvet altar cloth, shiny metal candlesticks, or a wool wall hanging as a backdrop will activate your sense of touch.

Are you using your altar to help create a significant new beginning or life direction? The numeral 1 is thought to be auspicious for new endeavors, so find one key object that is emblematic of your goal. If your new beginning involves veterinary school, you might want to place one piece of malachite on your altar to help with animal communication. If you're determined to lose weight, a single amethyst there may keep you motivated to stay on a diet. In general, onyx or another black stone facilitates renewal. Refer to the appendix for more information on the traditional meanings of numbers, gemstones, and flowers.

Many people place items on bedroom altars that they might be reticent to display in a more public space, such as a talisman or a statue of a saint or mythical deity. Totems also are frequent choices. These personifications of animals that represent different cosmic principles are especially important in Native American traditions but have been prominent in many cultures since ancient times. Their very antiquity gives them their strength. For example, an image of a frog inspires the courage to make a transformation that can lead to renewal. A hummingbird diffuses negativity and inspires one to live in the present, enjoying life as it is. A dolphin brings inner peace, harmony, and balance.

A totem may represent your clan or tribe, or you can adopt a personal animal totem. These spirit guides are said to enter and leave your life as you need them. An animal spirit may guide you along life's journey and teach you valuable lessons.

Your altar should balance light and darkness just as your room does. An easy way to illuminate your altar is with candles, or you can follow a tradition that harkens back to ancient times by using an oil lamp. For a more modern solution, install a light that can be dimmed or brightened. Another device that won't set your altar, your room, or your landlord's wrath alight (as candles and oil lamps might) is to purchase LED candles that look like votives. Some have a flicker button to add a touch of reality. If you prefer a real flame, keep it away from anything ignitable, like curtains and bedding. After concluding your meditation or other business, extinguish the flame. Carelessness with candles or incense burners is a primary cause of many house fires.

Your altar is a work in progress. It reflects your creative process, which shifts with your changing moods, wants, needs, and mental and spiritual growth. Altars can be permanent or portable. They can also be erected as shrines to honor relationships or one-time events, as you shall soon see.

Using Your Focal Point

Before you get started, bless your altar in a way that resonates with your spiritual beliefs. Some effective methods are to sprinkle it with salt and water, wave a candle flame over it, or cense with frankincense and myrrh. Some people associate those scents with spirituality because the resins are burned in Catholic churches and synagogues. Others rebuff those aromas because they bring up past negative experiences with organized religion. An alternative, especially for those who like an Asian flair, is sandalwood. Cedarwood, sage, and lavender are also traditional blessing incenses, especially for those attracted to Native American or Western Mystery traditions. The smoke has the added benefit of chasing away moths!

You can also anoint your altar cloth, candles, and sacred objects with perfumes and essential oils extracted from the substances mentioned above. If you want to try something different because you have a specific purpose in mind, visit a store that sells perfumes and experiment with samples until you find the right one. Rose makes a fine choice because of its high spiritual vibration and association with various spiritual paths over the ages. However, a woman I know detests the fragrance because it reminds her of her grandmother, with whom she has a less than cordial relationship. Speaking of roses, I advise against burning rose petals as incense because it smells disappointingly like burning leaves.

If you're not sure of what kind of incense or perfume to use, consult chapter 5. It includes short descriptions of traditional meanings associated with some time-honored scents. If you have an aversion to fragrances or are allergic, don't use them.

TEMPLE OIL

If you're still not sure of what kinds of essences to use, here's a formula for a general temple oil to anoint and bless your altar and the objects you place on it. Fill a dram vial with the following oils and shake well before using:

1 part Parvati sandalwood oil
1 part rose oil
1 part lotus blossom oil
4 drops lavender oil

Try acknowledging your altar every day. You don't need to meditate daily, although this is an excellent idea. A smiling "hello" greeting or a couple of minutes contemplating the beauty and purpose of this shrine will go a long way toward imbuing it with personal energy. With each passing day, the energy will grow until its powerful healing vibrations penetrate the furniture, walls, floors, and even the ceiling, strengthening you and your haven.

A Simple Window Altar

Maybe you don't have the room, permission, or money to erect a visible altar in your bedroom, but you do have a window. Why not design a focal point there? Windows are portals that separate the physical world from realms beyond. The light that windows let in is both physical and spiritual because it can illuminate the soul. Windows are also thought to carry our yearnings and petitions to the heavens. They represent hope, dreams, the desire to grow, and the courage to journey into the unknown, so they make perfect places for an altar.

One of the first things I do when I get up in the morning is to go to my bedroom window and look out at the sky, trees, birds, and squirrels cavorting in my garden and marvel at the stirring vision of the Front Range of the Rockies. Gazing out my window at this miracle of creation puts me in a happy, generous, and energetic mood. Even if your view is of a neighbor's wall, you can still see the sky, feel the movement of air, and listen to the sounds of the city, country, or suburb as they swirl around you, filling you with eagerness to prepare for the day ahead.

Transforming your bedroom window into an altar is easy to do, especially if the ledge is wide. If not, a small side table positioned against the wall under the window will suffice.

As with any altar, you can place your symbols there. Perhaps you'll also want to suspend a little bouquet of fragrant herbs from the curtain rod so the sun's warmth will release their scent into the room. Or hang a crystal, prism, or piece of stained glass so the sunlight striking it will send rainbows of refracted light into the room. An inexpensive alternative to stained glass is a press-on window decal of an ancient religious or philosophical symbol.

A word of advice: be extremely careful with open flames at a window altar. Even with the windows closed, a candle can cause a curtain to catch fire in an instant. This happened to friends of mine. They made it out of the house before it burned down, but their three Chihuahuas did not.

Activate your window shrine with a living plant. For example, an African violet with its neat purple or pink rosettes of blossoms is believed to open your third eye to spiritual insights. To harmonize yin/yang extremes in your personality, display a pink geranium or a plant associated with happiness and marriage like cyclamen. Grow a culinary herb in the window like marjoram to expand your worldview and open possibilities for travel. The light herbal aroma will perfume the room, and you'll have reaped the added reward of a fresh herb for cooking. Take a tip from the ancient Egyptians and meditate at your window altar at dawn, noon, sunset, and at night when the moon is climbing high in the sky to experience the effects of different kinds of light on your mind, emotions, and spirit.

Portable Focal Points

If you find it difficult to have a permanent focal point in your living arrangement, you can create a portable altar. Take all the items for your altar—including an altar cloth, candles, matches, perfumes, incense, and meaningful symbols—and pack them into a dresser drawer or store them in a box in the closet or under the bed. When you wish to use your altar, bring out the box, cover it with the altar cloth, and set everything you need on top of it. Here's a bonus: a portable altar won't collect dust the way permanent altars do.

Many of us spend a lot of time traveling from place to place. Times when you're in your vehicle, spending the night in a hotel in an unfamiliar city, or even commuting in the subway, train, or bus may be exactly those occasions when you most feel the need to visit your altar to slow down and regain peace of mind. When it isn't possible to retreat to your permanent safe harbor, the solution is to pack your portable altar. Of course, you'll need to modify it by whittling it down to essentials. Make it small enough to fit inside a makeup case or shaving kit, or even place it inside your wallet. In these matters, the size isn't as important as the energy you put into it.

A Mexican Wallet Shrine

Did I get your attention when I said you can carry a portable altar in your wallet? I suggest we look to Mexico for enlightenment. Mexicans have always been experts at creating crafts in miniature. The wallet shrine, an extension of this skill, depends on assiduous attention to detail.

This practice originated in Mexico and has expanded in popularity. In fact, wallet shrines, also known as wallet altars, have become so trendy that even if you've got two left thumbs when it comes to crafting, you can purchase one online at etsy.com. However, as with all things, I believe that putting your own energies into creating something for yourself reaps the maximum benefits. Your little wallet doesn't have to be perfect; what's important is that you designed and crafted it. Here's how to make one.

Cut a piece of plastic into a rectangular shape 5 inches long by 4 inches wide. Then make another, slightly smaller rectangle, 4 inches long by 3 inches wide, and a third one of the same size that ends in a triangle on one side. Next, cover the plastic on both sides with a brightly colored piece of sturdy cloth, and hand-stitch it together with yarn of a complementary color. For example, you might use red cloth and cyan yarn or a green-colored cloth and magenta yarn. Sew two sides to the central rectangle to create two flaps. Fold the rectangular flap inward and fold the one ending in a triangle over it. Then sew a snap on the two ends to keep the wallet closed. Presto! You've crafted a nifty basic wallet shrine.

If you're still having trouble getting the hang of it, go to www.thinkcrafts.com/blog/2009/06/12/how-to-make-a-wallet-shrine/. The blogger on this site makes a different style wallet that uses a lot of felt and little decorations that are often sold for scrapbooking. This site shows some good photos of the blogger's process.

When you open the sides, the shrine looks like a triptych with three divisions. Mexicans glue tiny, colorful pictures of saints, angels, Jesus, the Virgin of Guadalupe, crosses, sacred hearts, and other religious symbols to the cloth. Any given wallet shrine might include anywhere from three to twelve miniature pictures. Prayers and invocations handwritten in miniscule print may be pasted or stapled to the cloth. Finally, a small medal of a saint is attached to the top edge of the ensemble, directly in the middle. If your brand of spirituality doesn't encompass organized religion, feel free to substitute items like affirmations for prayers, miniature pictures of people you admire for saints, an ankh charm to represent life, an arrow pointing upward to show direction, or even tiny nature scenes. Include symbols that touch your heart.

Place the miniature shrine inside your wallet or carry it in your pocket or purse. Take it out at any time to meditate on its message or render a prayer. Think of bringing it along on an airplane, in your car, or even attached to the handlebar of your bike. When it's not in use, deposit it on your altar at home to absorb positive energy.

Single-Theme Altars

It is a sad fact of contemporary society that most of us have either witnessed or seen on the media spontaneous memorials that sprout up to honor those killed in mass shootings. Mourners leave floral tributes, teddy bears, balloons, and other items to honor those who tragically lost their lives. Or enter any teen's room, and chances are your vision will be bombarded by a wall plastered with photos of a favorite pop star or celebrity. Memorials and shrines like these are examples of single-theme altars. They have one purpose: to pay tribute to the subject. You can expand on this concept by generating your own temporary focal point for a specific reason. When you fulfill your goal, dismantle the altar and erect a new one for another goal. Here's an example.

A Wishing Wall Vision Board

My favorite single-theme altar story involves a wall. After Shawn and Alexa graduated from college in computer science, they were both offered good entry-level jobs at an up-and-coming software company in the city. They were thrilled with their exciting, challenging work and enjoyed meeting and socializing with fascinating new friends and colleagues. What they didn't like so much was that, for both economic reasons and housing availability, they had to live in a cramped studio apartment. They yearned for a house of their own, but given housing prices in the city and their modest incomes, they couldn't begin to pay the mortgage.

One rainy Sunday when they were both off work, they decided to construct a collage on the narrow hallway wall that ran between the studio and the bathroom. They cut out pictures of houses from magazines and books showing their idea of a dream home. They even tacked up floor plans and glossy photos of showcase gardens, bedrooms, kitchens, baths, and other living spaces.

The centerpiece to their construction arrived a couple of weeks later when Alexa, browsing at a vintage market, picked up a small crewelwork tapestry of an adorable country cottage. The little home had a thatched roof and a cobblestone walkway bordered by colorful hollyhocks, foxgloves, bluebells, and daffodils that led to an arched front door. Shawn fell in love with the little cottage, too, and they hung it in the middle of the collage. The couple called this makeshift vision board their "wishing wall" and often stood before it in rapt contemplation.

Six months passed, and both Alexa and Shawn were promoted and earning better salaries. Although they felt they could just about afford to buy a house now, nothing appeared on the horizon. Then one evening, Shawn arrived home late after an intense day at work. He noticed immediately that the collage and the little tapestry weren't in the dark hall. Alexa had moved it to a more prominent position on the well-lit wall facing their bed. Frustrated with the lack of action on finding a new home, she had decided to place the collage where they could focus on it more intently.

After dinner, they sat down and went over a lot of things having to do with their desire to move. They talked about exactly what it would be like living in a larger space farther away from work. What other sacrifices would they have to make? Would they keep the friends they'd made? Would they still be able to get into the city at night for entertainment? More topics emerged, and they discussed them all. Animated by their conversation, they resolved to be more consistent in visualizing their dream as coming true.

A month later, a friend of Shawn's from work invited the couple to a party at his cousin's house in a suburb. When they got out of the car, they almost fell over. The house next door was almost a dead ringer for the cottage in the tapestry. Only the roof was different, made of shakes, and the front door was painted blue, and the house was in a suburb, not the country. But the property was for sale! Three months later, after closing on the house, Shawn and Alexa moved to their dream home.

The concepts the couple used for their visioning board, albeit unknowingly, included clearly discerning their intentions, creating the right mix of images to display their objective, and finding the quintessential image in the tapestry. They moved the collage to a more central location so they could be consistent about repeatedly focusing on manifesting their dream.

As you finish reading this chapter, I suggest you concentrate on your dreams, needs, and preferences and ponder how to manifest them. Perhaps it will be by using an altar as a focal point, a vision board, or a wallet shrine. If you feel uncomfortable with formal altars, collages are not your thing, or shrines are too fussy for your taste, you don't need to follow all my suggestions. Use the ideas that make sense to you, fire your imagination, and give you joy.

five

The Fragrant Veil

This chapter is about the power of scent and how you can take advantage of the compelling qualities of incense and essential oils to enhance your sanctuary experience. If you're not a fragrance fan or are allergic, skip to chapter 6. Following is an example of how forcefully fragrance can affect the mind and emotions.

On one of my first trips to England, I was wandering down a cobblestone street in wet and windy Cambridge when I caught a whiff of burning incense. I couldn't tell whether the heady aroma was escaping from an open shop door, a church, or the window of a private home. In any case, it exerted a powerful effect on my emotions. The fragrance dissolved my cold discomfort and loneliness at being so far from my sunny Colorado home. My senses revived, and I was infused with a deep feeling of well-being. This is the power of incense: it calms yet invigorates while reaching to the furthest recesses of the psyche to excite the imagination.

A Pinch of Incense History

Our ancestors were attracted to aromatics, not only because burning fragrant substances masked the stench of animal sacrifices but also because naturally scented materials were, and still are, rare. Less than 5 percent of the world's plant species are aromatic, and so, to ancient societies, burning incense made a doubly fitting offering to their gods. The way the smoke curled up in spirals mimicked worshippers' entreaties traveling upward to the heavens and answers spiraling back down to earth.

Through empirical experimentation, ancient peoples also discovered something we are rediscovering afresh today: inhalation of aromatics can have profound healing effects on the human body. They performed incense fumigations of sickrooms using resins, gums, woods, and spices that today we know possess antibacterial, antifungal, and antiviral properties. Inhaling these aromas helped purify the patients' lungs and eliminate toxins from the immediate surroundings. So important was incense in the ancient world that societies mounted military campaigns to ensure that the precious raw materials necessary for creating aromatics would continue to flow smoothly over the Middle Eastern trade routes to the West.

Why Burn Incense in Your Sanctuary?

As my example at the beginning of this chapter illustrates, the sense of smell is often referred to as the silent sense because what you smell can affect your feelings, your mood, and even your physical reactions in subtle ways. How many times have you walked down the street around lunch or dinnertime and inhaled the aroma of roasting chicken, baking bread, or other culinary delights wafting from restaurants, store doorways, or an open window of someone's home? Did it make your mouth water? Of course it did. In a similar way, the aroma of burning incense can slow breathing, lower blood pressure, and even create a feeling of happiness, comfort, and peace of mind.

People burn incense in their sanctuaries for a variety of reasons. Aromatic smoke can aid concentration, facilitate meditation, induce a trance state, and hone the intuitive faculties. It can fumigate, purify, and protect; promote relaxation and aid sleep; stimulate romance; and simply make a fusty space more pleasant. If you really get serious about burning incense, you may see that it has a way of fostering personal renewal and spiritual growth, and maybe even stimulate communication with nature and the mysterious forces of the universe. Above all, burning incense can establish an atmosphere conducive to quiet thinking and meditation—something we all could do more of.

Incense Types

Some incenses are characterized as active. They are believed to command, attract, effect change, fumigate, and deodorize. Rosemary is one example. Other scents are considered passive and are burned to establish a spiritual, serene, relaxing, or sensual mood. Cheerful, apple-scented chamomile makes a superior passive incense. Be aware that some incenses—

such as datura, belladonna, mandrake, kava-kava, helle-bore, monkshood, and opium poppy—include hallucinogen-ic ingredients, many of which are illegal and therefore not widely available. Not to worry! You won't run across them at your local grocery or aromatherapy emporium.

Literally hundreds of differently fragranced incenses are available to purchase, but you don't have to make choosing the right kind a complex procedure. Three or four favorite "flavors" of stick incense, sold in many drugstores, gift shops, markets, or even at the supermarket, will probably provide an adequate selection for most occasions. For example, your cache might include vanilla for a happy home, rosemary to invigorate you, jasmine blossom for success, and frankin-cense for meditation. Cones (sometimes called punks) and pastilles (little square lozenges of incense) are also as simple to burn as the sticks.

Powdered Incense:
The Connoisseur's Choice

Sticks and punks are convenient to use, easy to store, and you don't need equipment other than a burner and match-es. However, true incense connoisseurs prefer powdered incense. The term *powdered* is something of a misnomer because rarely are the ingredients pulverized completely into powdered form. Usually little chunks of gums, resins, leaves, woods, flowers, and the like are mixed into a powder base. The final product appears somewhat chunky; therefore, it is also called loose incense. Loose incense snobs believe the difference between powdered and stick incense is rather like equating first flush Darjeeling loose tea to generic supermarket tea bags made from fannings and dust.

I admit that the high quality, potency, and variety of scents available in powdered form make a big difference if you're serious about burning incense. Another advantage of powdered incense is that you can add oils and botanicals to an already prepared formula to vary your theme, and you can use it as a sachet without burning it. The downside is it takes more time and effort to successfully and safely work with powders.

How to Burn Powdered Incense

In order to burn this type of incense, first you need to purchase special coals known as quick-burning, self-lighting, or quick-igniting. Coals are available at aromatherapy and mind-body-spirit stores, religious supply shops, and some groceries like Whole Foods. Made from willow wood and saltpeter, they generally come foil-wrapped in 40-millimeter (5 large coals) or 30-millimeter (10 small coals) sizes. You need to use this kind of coal because most loose incense is not self-igniting. Unlike stick incense, it doesn't contain saltpeter, which changes (in my opinion, adulterates) the aroma. I strongly advise against using barbecue coals because they emit noxious toxic fumes in the confined space of your home. However, you can always throw pinches of loose incense on a wood-burning fire, either in your fireplace or your outdoor clay chiminea.

Use any cauldron-style incense burner or a glazed clay pot with a wide mouth. If you prefer a metal burner, line it with fresh foil each time you use it so odors from previous burnings won't cling to the sides. Take care not to cover up the air holes necessary for the even burning of the coal. If you have a clay pot, fill it with sand, clean earth, small pebbles, or tiny shells to prevent it from cracking. If you use sand or dirt, make a few scratch marks in it to ensure smooth air flow beneath the coal. Scoop away the ash-covered base after each use. Add a new layer for the next time you light incense so it will burn cleanly without mingling aromas.

In the interest of safety, you might place a tile on the flat surface where you put the burner. Keep the burner away from furniture, curtains, rugs—anything flammable that a spark might ignite. An alternate inexpensive solution for a base is made from items you probably have at home. Cut a cardboard circle about a foot in diameter and cover it with tin foil. However, I'm not sure foil-covered cardboard is as solid and stable as a tile.

Now you're ready to place the coal in your burner and light it. If you bought the larger 40-millimeter coals, you may break one in half for economy's sake. I prefer to use the smaller, more convenient 30-millimeter size and place the whole coal in the burner.

The charcoal will catch fire immediately and sizzle as the saltpeter burns off in less than a minute. It will stay hot and glowing for around 30 minutes, giving you plenty of time to spoon very small amounts of incense on it. The operative phrase here is "very small amounts." Overdoing it will create too much smoke.

Use a tiny tin, silver, or glass spoon to deposit the incense. These are available from marijuana stores, antiques emporiums, specialty gourmet shops, tobacconists, or online. I use an aluminum spice scoop that looks like a Lilliputian shovel. Although not necessary, a miniature pair of tongs, like the ones used to pick up cubed sugar, is ideal for lifting a coal for a few seconds to encourage it to burn.

If you wish, continue to add bits of fresh incense until the coal is extinguished. Avoid accidents by never leaving your burner unattended while in use. After the burner cools, dispose of the ashes and foil, or remove the top layer of sand, earth, or pebbles.

To keep your coals from absorbing too much moisture, double-wrap them in aluminum foil and store them in an airtight box or resealable plastic bag with some silica gel beads (like the kind manufacturers place in a shoebox with a new pair of shoes) or use sand mixed with borax. If moisture eventually ruins a coal, do not despair. Try adding a drop or two of alcohol or perfume oil before lighting it.

Create Your Own Blends

Perhaps you're having trouble finding a supplier of loose incense or you may be the sort of person who enjoys crafting your own products. Putting together an incense blend is a bit like creating a potpourri or sachet, only you don't need to bother with specific colors, textures, fixatives, and spices. Instead, concentrate on gums, resins, botanicals, bases, and essential oils that release their fragrance when burned.

With practice, you can learn to blend personalized scents to fit your every need and desire.

When I make my own blends to sell through Caroline Dow Products, my online and mail order business, I like to start by placing in a mixing bowl the gums, resins, and woods I've crushed with a mortar and pestle. Next, I add the crushed botanicals, then the essential oils, blending well with each addition. Finally, I stir in the base, which holds the entire concoction together. More on bases in a moment.

Never use incense equipment for food preparation. Simply set your incense-making things aside. These will include a bowl, metal spoon for mixing, a set of measuring spoons and cups, and a glass jar to store your product. Metal equipment is easier to clean than plastic, and the ingredients won't penetrate metal as readily. You may also want to buy a mortar and pestle to crush botanicals. Although many ingredients are conveniently available in powdered form, crushing your own releases more of the essential oils. No matter what kind of equipment you choose, thoroughly clean it after each use or the aroma of one incense will mingle with another. Keep all ingredients and equipment out of the reach of children and pets.

Incense Ingredients

Here is a list of basic incense ingredients. In the interest of simplicity, I only include four ingredients in each category. Selecting one from each group will make a fine blend. Likewise, I've listed only one intention for each item, although many intentions are associated with each.

Gums and Resins

FRANKINCENSE (RESINOUS): prayer

MYRRH (WOODSY, RESINOUS): compassion

BENZOIN (RESINOUS, VANILLA-LIKE): self-confidence

COPAL (PINE-LIKE): positive change

Woods

CEDAR (WOODSY): regeneration

CINNAMON (SPICY): communication

SANDALWOOD (LIGHT, WOODSY): past-life recall

PINE (RESINOUS): fortitude

Berries

CUBEB (AROMATIC, PEPPERY): passion

JUNIPER (BITTER YET INVIGORATING): insomnia

BLACK PEPPER (PIQUANT, PUNGENT): alertness

ALLSPICE (SPICY, WARM): work performance

Peels

LEMON (CITRUSY, CLEAN): clarity

ORANGE (CITRUSY, MYSTERIOUS): success

TANGERINE (CITRUSY, SWEET): concentrated energy

BERGAMOT (FRESH, BALSAMIC): mood elevator

Seeds

ANISE (LICORICE): mind stimulant

CARDAMOM (SPICY, DRY): awakening

YELLOW MUSTARD (TANGY): protection

BASIL (HERBAL, PIQUANT): self-regeneration
   Note: Although I also use basil leaves, I've found
   that the dried seeds are quite potent and can be
   used throughout the winter.

Leaves

ROSEMARY (HERBAL, REFRESHING, RESINOUS):
   self-development

LAVENDER (REFRESHING): normalizer

EUCALYPTUS (REFRESHING, CAMPHOR-LIKE):
   purification

PEPPERMINT (REFRESHING): soothes nerves

Flowers

CHAMOMILE (APPLE-LIKE): inner peace

CLOVER (GRASSY, SWEET): good luck

MARIGOLD/CALENDULA (AROMATIC): lessens
   grief

CARNATION (SPICY, FLORAL): healing

Oils

JASMINE (FLOWERY, HEADY): antidepressant

ROSE (FLOWERY): harmony

NEROLI (FLOWERY): positive, directed energy

VANILLA (RICH, VANILLA-LIKE): inspiration

Bases

Commercially prepared pre-colored and pre-scented incense bases are convenient and smooth-textured. They quickly absorb oils and combine well with botanicals. However, the aromas sometimes leave something to be desired, being too cloying, at least to my sensitive nose. Also, bases can be difficult to obtain unless you have a resale license and can buy wholesale or find a retail supplier. Caroline Dow Products sells superior bases by the ounce via mail order and online at https://etsy.com/shop/CarolineDowProducts/.

Those who prefer to craft their own bases often use talc or a wood base. I advise against talc because inhaling it can harm your lungs. Wood base is a fancy name for sawdust. If you're handy with a saw, make the sawdust yourself. Otherwise, you can make a new friend by sweeping it up from a woodworker's shop floor. The wood base you collect—oak, pine, alder, fir, ash, etc.—depends on your preference for its aroma and its purpose and what the carpenter happens to have on hand.

If you want to color your incense, add dry tempera paint powders to your base. The amount will vary according to how much base you start with and how deep a color you want. The shades you can achieve in this way are endless, varying from light violet to chartreuse and golden orange to bright pink.

Cure your recipe for a week in an airtight glass container like a Ball canning jar, stirring every day until the oils are evenly absorbed. Be sure to label your jars because over time many incenses start to look alike.

Other Uses for Loose Incense

If you don't want to go to the bother of actually burning powdered incense, there are other ways you can use it. Powdered
incense is almost like a potpourri. It contains scent plus natural fixatives such as gums and resins. Fixatives help the fragrance remain true and not dissipate quickly. The most convenient way to use incense you're not going to burn is as a
sachet. Here are a few uses for incense sachets. Many more
exist, but the following will give you a start. Most of these
ideas come from folklore.

- Hold a small handful of the powder tight in
  your hand and throw it to the four winds before
  stepping over your threshold to help protect you
  from mishaps.

- Anoint the space between your eyebrows (known
  as the third eye) with incense to increase your
  awareness and intuition.

- Sprinkle it on a talisman, such as a favorite
  gemstone, and insert it with the stone into a
  small cloth bag. Carry the bag in your pocket or
  purse or hang it from your car's rearview mirror
  or above the inside of the door to your home for
  protection.

- Once again for protection, you can sprinkle bits
  of incense in the corners of your sanctuary or
  home.

- Use the sachet to perfume your closet or clothing
  drawers to delight you every time you breathe
  it in. I keep a couple of lavender sachets in my

clothing drawers to help the clothes stay fresh and clean smelling.

- If your incense sachet is comprised of cedarwood, southernwood, feverfew flowers, and lavender, you can place it in your clothes or linen closet to chase away moths and other annoying bugs.

As a final note on incense, I'd like to mention that according to folklore, the way incense smoke blows is said to portend positive or negative events. If the smoke blows to the right, all is well; if to the left, not so much. If it blows away from you, a bad situation will pass over; if it blows toward you, then good times are in store. If it blows both to the left and right, conditions are unsettled and caution is advised. Then again, it might just blow around because of a draft!

Essential Oils for Your Sanctuary

One of my clients who sees me for personal fragrance consultations once complained that her landlord made her quit burning loose incense because it set off the smoke alarm. I explained that she probably went overboard and burned too much at a time—something that's easy to do. I suggested that she consider burning stick incense instead because unless it's lighted directly under a smoke detector, it won't set it off.

Still, I understood her point. Not to mention that the aroma probably penetrated to adjoining apartments, which might not be appreciated by other residents. I also know that many people who would like to use scent in their sanctuaries suffer from diseases like asthma or are allergic to smoke. So for my client and those others, I recommend essential oils.

Essential oils, also known as essences, are volatile oils extracted from botanicals by a number of methods and used in perfumery, aromatherapy, and herbal medicine. These plant-based substances have complex chemical structures, with some containing over 100 components, and this is how they work.

The cerebral cortex registers smells, but fragrant substances bypass this area of the brain and zoom directly to the limbic system. The limbic system is very old and developed long before humans learned to perform higher brain functions like analysis. Our perception of the fragrances inherent in essential oils is immediate and unconscious because analysis from other parts of the brain doesn't get into the act.

Because aromas affect us on deep levels, they help eliminate the emotional propensities locked in the limbic system that can lead to disease and discomfort. Essential oils automatically release beneficial chemicals into the brain like endorphins, which are the same substances that make runners and other athletes feel good after a workout. Essences stimulate other chemicals like serotonins, which help relax and tranquilize. Encephalins block pain, slow breathing and the heartbeat, and promote digestion. Pheromones activate the sex drive, and noradrenaline helps keep a person alert and motivated.

All of this makes essential oils ideal for healing, renewal, and spiritual purposes. This science of healing is called aromatherapy. You can anoint your altar, symbolic objects, and even yourself with these aromatherapeutic oils or, if you prefer, heat them in an aroma diffuser.

Essences are typically divided into ten different categories according to types of scent. While scores of oils fall into each category, there's only room here to list one of each kind. If you get super enthusiastic about using aromatherapeutic oils in your sanctuary, I recommend you read books dedicated to the subject or take an aromatherapy class.

Following are ten scents, one from each fragrance category, followed by their aromas in parentheses. Next come the aromatherapeutic properties, ending with some spiritual uses for your haven.

NEROLI (FLOWERY): This orange-scented oil calms anxiety, stress, fear, and heart palpitations, and deodorizes. It is considered a sexually magnetic scent. Neroli brings peace and harmony to the home and transforms confused, nervous, or negative energy into a directed, serene, positive force. Use it for meditations to focus on attenuation of grief. This essence also stimulates the heart chakra and psychic centers.

LEMON BALM (CITRUSY): Also known as Melissa, this lemony fragrance possesses sedative qualities to ease nervous tension and combat insomnia and migraines. It's also an antiviral. Meditate with this fragrance when you are faced with having to speak in public as it is said to confer eloquence. Lemon balm is also used in meditations to facilitate both past-life recall and predict future events.

CHERRY (FRUITY): The sweet scent of cherry blossom helps improve academic performance because it promotes the desire to be better educated and more spiritually aware. Use it in the home to foster a light-hearted environment and in meditations to attain your heart's desire.

EUCALYPTUS (GREEN, REFRESHING): A clean-smelling essence, eucalyptus breaks up congestion from head and chest colds and asthma. Use it to purify your sanctuary and home (I add it to my laundry wash cycle) and to nurture good health. It's an ingredient of many creams and lotions to alleviate rheumatoid arthritis and muscle pain. Eucalyptus is toxic in high doses. Do not ingest.

ROSEMARY (HERBY, STIMULATING): The oil extracted from this popular herbal bush is an antiseptic and fumigant. In aromatherapy it is an ingredient of cleansing washes, rejuvenation lotions, and creams to preserve youth. Rosemary is also a nerve stimulant that improves the memory and blood circulation. The scent is thought to help banish nightmares and attract friendly ghosts. Use it in meditations to aid psychic self-development and to acquire serenity and wisdom. This essence is not recommended for epileptics or during pregnancy.

CLOVER (GRASSY, MELLOW): Clover is an alterative that gradually restores health and vitality. It is used in aromatherapy to prevent spasms, ease bronchial congestion, and shrink ovarian cysts and fibroids. By tradition, it's used in meditations to draw good fortune and success, encourage faithfulness, and protect travelers.

CINNAMON (SPICY): Besides being a spicy culinary ingredient, cinnamon is a germicide that kills the typhoid bacillus. It's an effective agent against genito-urinary tract and intestinal infections, calms coughing spasms, and combats lice. Uses in your meditations include altar purification, blessing, prosperity, psychic awareness, abundance, trade, communication, and creativity. Both the leaf and bark are skin irritants, so dilute them before using. Cinnamon is convulsive in large doses.

PATCHOULI (ANIMAL, SEXUAL): This long-lasting scent is a nerve stimulant in small doses but sedative in large amounts. It's also an astringent, tissue rejuvenator, and fungicide. Meditate with patchouli to attract love, prosperity, and the power of the gnomes, the elemental spirits of earth.

SANDALWOOD (WOODSY, MOSSY): Sandalwood has many uses in aromatherapy. It's an antiseptic remedy for genito-urinary tract infections and helps heal colic, gastritis, laryngitis, hemorrhoids, nausea, and chapped skin. This oil is also a heart tonic and antidepressant. Use it in meditations that require a good deal of concentration or if you engage in past-life recall. It's a relaxing, grounding fragrance that encourages openness.

BENZOIN (RESINOUS, FIXATIVE): Although it's a resin, benzoin smells a lot like vanilla. This essential oil increases blood circulation and urine flow. It's antifungal and soothing for chapped red skin. The fragrance is used in meditations for self-growth and increased self-confidence and to counteract loneliness and sadness by strengthening the heart chakra and bringing peace of mind.

An Ounce of Prevention

For our purposes in this book, you'll mainly use essential oils to anoint candles, altar cloths, robes, and objects for your altar or use them in an aroma diffuser during meditations and contemplations. However, some readers may also wish to anoint their temples, the space between the brows on the forehead (the third eye), wrists, ankles, etc. For you, or for anybody who handles these oils, here are a few words of caution:

- You may be allergic to a particular oil, so always perform this skin patch test before using. Mix a couple drops of essence with ½ teaspoon of a carrier oil, such as grapeseed, sweet almond, jojoba, or coconut. Apply the mixture to the inside of your forearm. Reactions occur within a few minutes up to a couple of hours.

- Never take essential oils internally as a substitute for seeing a doctor. If you ingest essential oils for medicinal purposes, I highly recommend you do so under the guidance of a licensed aromatherapist or physician.

- Do not use known irritant oils in the bath.
- Do keep all oils out of reach of children and pets.
- Essential oils that may irritate the skin include bay rum, birch, black pepper, cinnamon bark, cinnamon leaf, citronella, clove bud, clove leaf, cumin, lemongrass, oregano, peppermint, pimento, savory, red thyme, and thuja.
- Essential oils for external use only: bitter almond, arnica, calamus, eucalyptus, hyssop, mimosa, mugwort, nutmeg, oakmoss, sassafras, tonka bean, thuja, tuberose, and all synthetics (fragrances concocted from chemicals in a laboratory).
- Oils not to be used by children or pregnant or nursing women: aniseed, armoise, basil, bay, birch, cajeput, camphor, cedar, clary sage, clove bud, clove leaf, coriander, fennel, jasmine, juniper, myrrh, oregano, pennyroyal, peppermint, pimento berry, red thyme, rosemary, sage, savory, spearmint, and tarragon.
- Photosensitizing oils that make the skin more sensitive to harmful ultraviolet rays: angelica, bergamot, carrot, cumin, lemon, lime, and orange.

six

Your Bathroom
As the Ultimate Retreat

To help complete the idea of your entire home as a haven, let's start with one of the most underrated but intensely personal areas—your bathroom.

For many people, bathrooms epitomize the concept of a sanctuary. The bathroom can be a place of refuge, a place where you can engage in meditation and contemplation undisturbed. Bathrooms are also associated with water symbolism and bathing.

Water Power

Our world and our bodies are composed primarily of water, which profoundly influences our physical and emotional states as well as the subconscious mind. This is why undines, mermaids, mermen, and kelpies—mythical creatures of fairy tales and myths—are accredited with the power to mesmerize.

Our ancestors highly valued water and took great care constructing bathing facilities. The oldest known bathroom was built six thousand years ago in India. In some areas of Iraq, people still use fifteen-hundred-year-old toilets and sewer systems. Do you suppose the plumbing in your house will last as long?

The art of bathing in ancient times reached its high-water mark during the Roman era. The Romans' idea of a bathing facility was very different from ours. Their baths were like small towns with gaming rooms, libraries, art galleries, meeting facilities, and temples that would put our contemporary health clubs to shame. The baths at Caracalla, Italy, built in 217 CE, held up to eight thousand bathers at a time and had cold- and hot-water therapy pools and exercise rooms. I guess Poppaea, Emperor Nero's wife, didn't care much for crowds because she bathed daily on her own—and not in water but in scented she-asses' milk.

The quality and quantity of bathrooms in many American homes has improved markedly over the years. Most of us have left behind the one-hole outhouses and single bathroom for the entire family, who only bathed on Saturday nights to conserve water. Nowadays, people aspire to bedroom-size bathrooms complete with gigantic soaking tubs, separate multi-headed showers, Jacuzzis, hot tubs, saunas, and even entertainment centers. And when we tire of frolicking in our own bathrooms, we book a vacation to a hot spring or spa where we can be pampered on the same scale as Empress Poppaea was. All this just goes to show that in one way or another, we've fallen under the spell of those undines and mermaids of ancient lore.

Create Your Personal Spa

You may not be able to afford a hot tub, Jacuzzi, or a trip to a hot spring, but you can make a personal spa out of your bathroom. If you own your home and can do whatever you like with the bathroom, here are some ideas. If you can't decorate in a permanent fashion, a portable beauty chest, which I describe later in this chapter, works just as well.

Like a spa, your bathroom sanctuary should engage all your senses. For the sense of sight, you might decorate with symbols of the sea such as mermaids, seashells, seahorses, starfish, or sea animals like dolphins and seagulls. In my bathroom I've placed a blue glass pelican. A plant that reminds you of the ocean, such as an indoor palm, also looks elegant. Many indoor plants thrive in humidity, so you will be doing your plant a favor, too. If you want to go all out, install a fish tank and fill it with colorful fish.

Choose a color scheme from the cool end of the spectrum to evoke water. Blue, green, violet, purple, silver, and white all make appropriate choices. For sound, play nature music or water sounds. Place a stone under the sink faucet and turn it on to a slow drip; alternatively, install a sink top water feature. For texture and to filter the light, cover the window and tub with diaphanous, filmy, or lacy material or hang a shimmering beaded curtain.

Scent is probably more important here than in any other room. You have lots of choices, and what you select depends on your fragrance preferences. You can do aroma diffusers, bath bags, bath bombs, bath salts, body lotions, colognes, essential oils, potpourris, and scented candles. A word of advice: don't mix too many different scents together or they will compete and cancel each other out. Besides, your nostrils may get overwhelmed. Traditional relaxing aromas are lavender and rose. Vanilla creates harmony and balance, and eucalyptus eases tired muscles. To make you feel like you're walking on a summer beach, select a fragrance that includes either bay rum, lime, narcissus, or sandalwood.

For a sensuous experience, choose animal fragrances like musk or civet. In this instance, synthetics are better than pure essential oils because they don't harm or kill animals. To enliven your blend, add a pinch of spice to the aroma, such as allspice, cardamom, clove, or nutmeg.

You may enjoy smelling scent in the air but not so much on your body. If so, use an aroma diffuser or place potpourri or a scented candle in the bathroom. If smells are not your thing, don't use them. Simply bathing in a pleasant environment is enough.

Don't forget to bring in fluffy slippers and towels, a bath pillow to cradle your head, and a comfy bath rug for the floor. After all, you have set aside this time and place to treat yourself to comfort and luxury so you can face life's challenges afresh. Don't feel guilty about indulging yourself; you're worth it!

A Writer's Bathroom Retreat

If you're ready to turn your bathroom into a sanctuary but need further guidance, here's an example of how one woman fashioned a bathroom sanctuary that stimulates her creative juices.

My writing mentor, Barbara Steiner, has authored more than sixty books. Her bathroom retreat reflects her highly developed imagination along with her love of nature and wry sense of humor. Barbara claims her "froggy bathroom," as she calls it, evolved of its own accord. The room, though small, has two east-facing windows with a turquoise-blue sunken tub in front of them. The original tub gave Barbara and her husband the notion to build moss rock around the tub and halfway up two walls. They bought a matching toilet and two silver basins, which they nestled into a shiny black bathroom counter. They finished the basics by covering the floor in grayish-black slate to mimic the ground outdoors.

The moss needs to be sprinkled with water from time to time to keep it alive. Barbara doesn't mind performing this chore because the moss makes the tub feel like a natural pool carved from rocks deep within a forest.

To further enhance the woodland ambience, she's surrounded her tub with a leafy philodendron, an enormous umbrella plant, and a few hanging plant baskets that form a green canopy over the tub. Bamboo window coverings add texture and can be raised or lowered depending on how much light she wants to let in. Large mirrors on two walls reflect light into the room, giving it a spacious feeling. When

Barbara bathes in the evenings, she either turns on the make-up bulbs around the mirrors or lights a few candles that emit a slight woodsy scent.

The frogs materialized when Barbara realized that this indoor-outdoor environment would make an ideal home for them. Although she couldn't have live frogs in the bathroom, she could do ceramic substitutes. The first one she fell in love with was a Buddha frog she bought because of its quixotic expression. Her collection grew to include souvenirs of her world travels and gifts from friends and family. Some are hewn from native stone, like the Italian rana. The Mexican frogs have miniature cultural scenes painted on their backs, while the ceramic frogs with wide-open mouths are made by a Colorado potter. She's even collected a froggy doubles tennis team that reflects her favorite sport.

In this restful place, Barbara lies back in the tub, soaks away her troubles, gazes out the windows to the treetops, and watches the birds and squirrels romp in her garden. The tub is also one of her favorite places to dive into a novel or volume of poetry. She keeps a pad of paper and pen nearby to capture ideas for writing from her subconscious. She says, "Relaxation sends me into my right brain, which is where the good ideas come from."

Barbara counsels those who want to construct a similar sanctuary to first create a vision of what they want. She suggests thinking about what soothes you and feeds your soul. Blue and green make her feel particularly good, but she understands everyone reacts differently to colors. She also advises to always be aware. "If you see a place you like," she suggests, "identify what attracts you and see if you can incorporate its features into your own space."

She believes that you don't need to establish your haven all at once. "Start with one object as a focal point, as I did with my tub. Over time, pick and choose the objects you want to build around it. Sanctuaries are very personal; they should reflect your individuality."

Make a Portable Beauty Chest

"Remodeling your bathroom is fine for those who have the money and are single," you may say, "but I share my bathroom with my sister, her significant other, and another housemate." If you can't refashion your bathroom, you can bring in a portable beauty chest to transform it temporarily. Find a large, attractive container or make one from a sturdy box and cover it with silvery paper, symbolic of the water element. If you're gifted with an artistic flair, paint symbols of beauty on the box like flowers, fans, Victorian hats, ornate slippers, perfume bottles, the astrological Venus symbol, gloves embellished with pearls and feathers—whatever evokes beauty and femininity for you. An alternative would be to cut pictures from magazines and glue them to the silvery paper along with sequins and glitter.

Tuck inside a couple of small candlesticks, appropriate candles for the kind of meditation you want to perform, and a length of muslin, silk, or other soft cloth to drape over the counter and/or toilet. Complete your beauty chest with bath products, emollients, incense, burner, and matches. And while you bathe, don't forget a piece or two of your favorite sweet, such as a chocolate truffle or a luscious caramel, which will engage the sense of taste. Keep your beauty chest well stocked to use when spending time away from home to relax and comfort you.

A Healing Bath

You've got your refuge arranged the way you like; now what to do with it? For openers, try taking a bath. Do I hear a murmur of protest? Are you saying that, like so many people in our hectic contemporary society, you don't have time to luxuriate in the bath? Maybe it's one reason we're a pretty frazzled bunch.

You don't take a bath simply to be self-indulgent. Baths heal both body and soul, and obviously you understand that you need to recharge your batteries or you wouldn't be reading this book. The bath is one of the easiest places to meditate because not only is it absolutely private, the very act of undressing in this quiet space is conducive to withdrawal into one's subconscious thoughts.

The warm water lapping around your body will soothe tired, sore muscles, calm your nerves, and rejuvenate your skin. The skin is the largest organ of the body, twice the weight of either the liver or the brain. It protects you from pollution and injuries, helps you breathe, and excretes toxins. Skin also regulates your internal temperature and provides you with strong sensory stimuli. With all of these benefits going for it, your skin deserves extra attention by soaking it.

To excrete maximum toxins and stimulate circulation, add Epsom salts, sea salt, or Himalayan salts to your bath water. For a soothing bath, top it off with a few drops of relaxing essential oils like those listed in the last chapter.

A SERENITY BATH BAG

Now that I've convinced you of the benefits of bathing, here's a recipe for a Serenity Bath Bag that I've developed to enrich your meditation sessions. Use a small muslin bag or, if you can't find one, a piece of muslin, which you can tie together with a ribbon so the ingredients don't spill out. All the herbs should be dried. In a bowl, place the following ingredients and mix well:

1 tablespoon old-fashioned oatmeal
1 teaspoon hops
½ teaspoon rosemary
½ teaspoon lavender
½ teaspoon Roman chamomile
½ teaspoon linden flowers and bracts
½ teaspoon valerian
½ teaspoon rose or jasmine oil
½ teaspoon tangerine oil
⅛ teaspoon French lavender oil

Spoon the ingredients into the bag. Bath bags are really only good for one use, so you might want to make up a larger amount in advance if you intend to use a bath bag often. You can reuse the empty muslin bag if you wish.

If you don't care for this combination of aromas, concoct your own blend or buy one to correspond to your meditation topic. If you can't think of a good theme, try one associated with the concept of water such as cleansing, regeneration, creativity, fluidity, receptivity, the female force, intuition, compassion, or divination.

Some people prefer not to mess around with oatmeal and herbs in the bath or really don't want to absorb the concoction into their skin. If this is you, here's a formula you can put into your aroma diffuser. Place only a couple drops of the blend at a time into the diffuser and check the manufacturer's directions. The following is a general recipe, but it's also good for solving a problem in the tub in the section that follows.

INNER GUIDE OIL BLEND

20 drops sandalwood oil
10 drops frankincense oil
8 drops honeysuckle oil
4 drops lily of the valley oil

Place in a dram vial, cover with a lid, and shake vigorously before placing a couple of drops into the diffuser. As with the bath bag, you can make up larger amounts initially to keep a little stock of the formula.

Solve a Problem in the Bath

In spite of our best intentions, sometimes we simply don't have the time or energy to take a bath and add a meditation to it. For those times, here's a meditation to perform with or without the addition of a bath. If you want to do it without bathing, simply place two lighted blue candles on the bathroom sink and sit on the toilet (with the lid down) or on a chair. To replicate the watery environment of the tub, turn on the faucet to a slow drip. Alternatively, play nature sounds that mimic pattering raindrops. If you're lucky, you can also perform this meditation when it is actually raining outside so you can hear the drops falling on your roof or the ground.

If you prefer to meditate in the tub, choose to take your bath at a time when your children, spouse, siblings, or roommates aren't likely to disturb you. And turn off your phone! Reserve a half hour in the tub and fifteen minutes after bathing to complete the meditation and your ablutions.

Purchase two blue votive candles. Affix the candles in votive holders, light, and place them on either side of the faucet. If you're really enthusiastic about this meditation, you can draw the symbol of a crescent moon, a water symbol, on a piece of cardboard. Paint it silver, cut it out, and tape it to the wall at the end of the tub so you face it when you lie back. If you enjoy scent, burn a stick of sandalwood or jasmine incense.

Draw a warm bath (98 to 105 degrees Fahrenheit), and add some of the inner guide oil to the water. Position your bath pillow to support your neck and head. If you don't have a pillow, make one by folding a soft towel to place under your head and neck. Get into the tub, lie back, and relax.

From time to time, let your gaze turn to the lighted candles. If any current niggling issue rears its ugly head, mentally grab it and thrust it deep into the water. Sometimes an idea of how to solve your problem will occur while you're watching the candles. In this case, mentally capture the possible solution in your mind's eye and stick it onto the candle with your thoughts. Go on to your next thought and repeat the process.

Eventually, no more thoughts will occur to you. This means your mind and body have profoundly relaxed. This thought-free, stress-free state is what you're aiming to achieve. You can't force relaxation; it just happens. You're now ready to access your inner guide.

If you don't feel totally at ease after thirty minutes, don't obsess. Trust the essences in the bathwater to work with your inner guide to create subtle changes in your body, your aura, and your chakras. An aura is the psychic energy field or invisible emanation alleged to surround people, plants, animals, and inanimate objects. Chakras are the nerve centers that align with the central nervous system.

When time's up, pull the plug on the water and step out of the tub. As you dry off and dress, visualize your problem flowing down the drain with the bathwater. Carry the lighted votives to your room—encased in two washcloths so as not to burn your fingers on the hot glass—and place them on your bedroom altar, if you have one.

Write in a notebook or your journal the possible solutions to your problem as well as considerations from your inner guide that surfaced. If you've forgotten some of the ideas already, for inspiration, look to the candles where you mentally stuck your solutions. If you still don't remember, it's likely the answers will occur in a dream or in another bath. Occasionally refer back to your bath-solutions notebook. You'll be amazed at how, over time, you've managed to come up with the right ways to solve your problems.

Thank whatever higher power you believe in for the insights, and extinguish the candle flames with a snuffer.

Aren't you happy you made time to take a bath?

seven

Forging a Haven
in Your Kitchen

Now that your bath has relaxed and revitalized you, let's move on to a more challenging space—one which, with a little attention, can also become an amazing sanctuary. Kitchens are more than convenient places to prepare and consume meals. In former times, these beehives buzzed with domestic activity. With its constantly burning hearth fire, the kitchen was the warmest room in the house, so it doubled as a nursery, schoolroom, and a bedroom when an occupant fell ill. The family gathered there to enjoy meals, gossip, and spin yarns late into the night. Nowadays in the United Kingdom, households with AGA cookers—a cast-iron heat-storage stove—can experience a similar warm and cozy feeling.

Feng shui gurus claim that the kitchen represents the heart of the household, its palpitating energy center. In contemporary American society, many homeowners seem to agree with this assessment. They have their homes built with an all-encompassing great room that usually includes a kitchen that opens to it. And have you ever noticed at parties that guests seem to congregate in the kitchen, even if it's a narrow space the size of a camper van kitchen, while the beautifully decorated living room stands virtually empty? Somehow, people intuitively feel this room's vital force and are drawn to it. For this reason, this corner of the home merits the utmost respect. And by applying a little thought and elbow grease, you can transform yours into a personal haven.

Just because the entire family gathers there doesn't mean you can't put your personal stamp on your kitchen. The homemaker has always held undisputed reign over this precinct, and I'm no exception to the rule. My husband doesn't even know which pot goes where! To illustrate my point, here's a variation on the adage "Too many cooks spoil the broth," taken from my own experience living in Scotland.

At the time, I was staying in a widower's sixteenth-century ancestral home. One night I prepared dinner for him and several guests. This tradition-bound gentleman wouldn't allow anyone else in the kitchen while I was cooking, even though I could have used help dealing with the dated appliances in that vast space. He told me that his mother had laid down this rule. Constant intrusions would interfere with her concentration and might cause her to spoil and throw away an entire meal—something unthinkable for the pennywise Scots. The widower would never have understood my own kitchen, which has six doors through which anybody can pass at any time and often do.

As your sanctuary guide, here's some advice: never buy a house with six doors to the kitchen. Besides the door problem, I'd say "fat chance" to the opportunity of ever getting enough peace and quiet in my kitchen to prepare a meal unhindered. Everything, including the proverbial kitchen sink, ends up in this room, from bicycle wheels and school play costumes to power drills and kitty litter bags. The front of the refrigerator is plastered with reminder notes, children's artwork, family photos, restaurant coupons, and postcards from friends who have traveled to exotic lands I'll probably never visit. Nevertheless, my kitchen is a cheery, vibrant space often overflowing with friends and loved ones engaging in lively discussions.

After the house quiets down at night, I reclaim hegemony over my space. Sitting at the kitchen table in peaceful solitude, I sip a cup of chamomile, honey, and vanilla tea and contemplate the day's events and sometimes even the meaning of life and the splendor of the universe.

A Sanctuary in Progress

Here are some ideas on how to turn your kitchen into a sanctuary in progress. I say "in progress" because within a twenty-four-hour span, it probably goes from clean to cluttered, messy, and just plain dirty. When you feel the need to reestablish control, your first step is to tidy up well. In many cultures, brooms stand for spiritual cleansing, so be sure to sweep the floor with a broom instead of using a vacuum. Next, scrub the floor with white vinegar and water. Besides being an effective cleaner, Vodou practitioners believe that vinegar purifies spiritually by banishing evil spirits and impure thoughts.

On a nice day, open a window or door. If your budget permits, freshen the environment with cut flowers and hang herbs to dry on the high space over the sink. Burn a stick of culinary spice incense, like cinnamon, vanilla, or clove, or set an open bowl of fragrant potpourri on the counter. You can also try a trick I learned from a real estate agent. She said that when you put your house up for sale, you should grind a few fresh citrus peels in the disposal. A sweet, citrusy scent will permeate the air to eliminate cooking odors and lend a homey ambience.

Refrigerator Door as Easel

One way to personalize your kitchen and create an activity that your family can enjoy is to use your refrigerator door as an easel to display art. Minimalist kitchen decorator consultants advocate keeping the door clutter-free to encourage you to maintain a pristine kitchen and an uncluttered mind. I agree with this recommendation if you're selling your home. Personally, I prefer not to leave the space completely blank. For me, blank spaces equate with blank minds. You might try compromising by attaching a single item on the door such as a picture of a goal you wish to achieve or an inspirational landscape. This way, you focus on your ideal every time you open the fridge door and perhaps meditate on it when you have time. After all, with the exception of your main entrance, this door probably receives the most action.

On the other end of the spectrum are those who personalize their refrigerator doors to such an extent that an entire category called Refrigerator Art has emerged. Kids' Refrigerator Art competitions, whether drawn on paper and attached to the door or painted directly on the appliance, are popular. Connoisseurs of Adult Refrigerator Art have paid up to $5,000 for prime examples. Think of the new fridge you could buy for that kind of money! In San Diego, the Institute for Arts Education conducts classes on Refrigerator Art for children to nurture their creativity.

If the concept of refrigerator door as easel appeals to you and your family, I encourage you to use it to create a meaningful sacred space for all.

Thai Dining Traditions to Guide You

As the homemaker or at least the one who prepares most meals, you're in charge of making this communal sacred space a comfortable, congenial dining experience for your household. For some tips on how to accomplish this, let's turn to the people of Thailand. Thais equate happiness with a full tummy. This is why many of their important customs center on food and eating. Thais don't schedule mealtimes. Instead, they eat small amounts throughout the day and evening.

These snacks, or little meals, are served on a long teakwood table in a room that is open on all sides to take advantage of the cooling cross breezes in the warm climate. Thais generally put in hours of meal preparation, partly because they like to orchestrate elaborate presentations along with pretty table decorations. They arrange the food on very small plates often made of celadon green glass. The china's gentle spring-like color resonates harmoniously with nature, which is important to Thais. They artfully tuck bronzeware eating implements into folded napkins. Vases overflowing with tropical flowers such as lotus, orchids, and birds of paradise add a delicate wash of color to the setting. The tempting food and the care taken in its presentation create a convivial space.

I realize that most of us in our busy contemporary Western societies can't or won't take time to choreograph such complex meals. Still, we all can benefit from some of the tips provided by these Asians. I imagine your dining area isn't open air, but on a warm evening, you can mobilize your kitchen and serve dinner on the patio, balcony, or in your backyard. It will make an entertaining change for everybody.

A teakwood table in the kitchen may not fall within your budget or decorating plan, but you can modify the idea by purchasing a solid oak table with wide, comfortable matching dining chairs. Instead of gobbling down their food and taking off to other commitments, perhaps your family members will relax, take their time eating (always good for their health), and chat about the day's events and what's on their minds. When I lived in Britain, I noticed many families, whether they resided in a country manor house or in a small city flat, strived to have a big solid table in their kitchens for family gatherings.

You may not have time or inclination for Thai-style intricate food preparations, but even cooked frozen pizza served on pretty china with separate sides of garlic bread and salad makes a charming meal. If the salad is colorful and cleverly arranged on elegant plates instead of on microwavable plastic, little Izzy might even eat it.

As to decorations, even plastic knives, forks, and spoons can look nice when tucked into a napkin folded into the shape of a swan or a pocket. Such arrangements only take a few minutes to create, and you'll get better with practice. For instructional videos, my favorite sites are on Martha Stewart (https://www.marthastewart.com/1112146/how-to-fold-a-napkin-ways?) and at Buzz Feed (https://www.buzzfeed.com/peggy/28-creative-napkin-folding-techniques-for-every-oc).

A bouquet picked from the garden or a dried flower arrangement can also beautify the dining table (I know that feng shui experts will disagree about dried flowers, but they are convenient). Don't forget fragrance, if you like it. Burning vanilla- or cinnamon-scented candles or incense can create a harmonious ambiance conducive to pleasant social interaction.

Thais listen to the bells and chants from ever-present nearby monasteries while they eat. You can play easy listening music. I suggest you avoid talk shows and television, though, or your companions will tend to listen or watch rather than communicate with each other. In these ways, you can adapt Thai dining customs to your situation and upgrade your kitchen's sanctified space.

Other Kitchen Traditions and Superstitions

Because almost everyone cooks, all kinds of traditions and superstitions have grown up around cooks and their kitchens in cultures worldwide. Here are a handful of examples to amuse you and perhaps adapt to your setting.

Hindus treat the kitchen as the most hygienic room of the house because to do otherwise might incur the wrath of their gods (not to mention a fiesta of bacteria). On entering the dining area, they leave their shoes outside the door and sprinkle water around the room as a nod to their ancestors. You can perform a variation on this tradition by dipping a clean dishtowel in water with a few drops of sandalwood, orange, or another pleasant-smelling essential oil. Make sure the water contains a true essence rather than a synthetic so it doesn't leave a stain on the furniture, carpet, or table linens. Wave the wet towel around the room to distribute the droplets. You'll bless your dining space and make it smell heavenly, too.

Another kitchen custom originates in the Candomblé religion practiced in Brazil and some parts of Africa. To balance the meal with the natural rhythms of nature by moving in the direction in which the sun is perceived to pass through the sky, the cook always stirs the pot clockwise, never counterclockwise. She also sings songs of praise while preparing the food to obtain the gods' blessings. When the repast is ready, she retreats from the room, never turning her back on the offering as a sign of respect for the gods, who provide sustenance. While I don't encourage you to follow this procedure,

I do think that if you hum a merry tune while you cook or listen to happy music, your culinary tasks will probably conclude more swiftly and pleasantly.

Here's an old English tradition you can follow to assure that your kitchen activities tool along seamlessly, without any culinary disasters. Place a piece of bread on a white saucer and pour honey and milk over it. Put the saucer on the stove as an offering to the Hob, a kind of stove fairy. Although this remedy might sound outlandish, you might consider it the next time you're faced with cooking a last-minute Thanksgiving dinner for twenty people.

So many superstitions are centered around food and cooking that it would take an entire book to list them all. For example, to drop a knife spells bad luck, but if you drop a spoon and it lands upside down, it means you're about to get a surprise. Spilled milk, especially on the threshold, is alleged to attract fairies. And you should never throw away a piece of bread unless you want your luck to go into the garbage with it.

So-called lucky foods are associated with each month of the year. They include peas in January, noodles in February, edible seeds in March, eggs in April, yogurt in May, cake in June, watermelon in July, corn in August, oysters in September, pumpkin pie in October, turkey in November, and dried fruit in December. Probably many of these alleged fortunate foods came about because of seasonal availability and associations with different holidays.

Grape Juice Meditation

By now, your kitchen should be as clean and sparkling as a sunny summer morning. Time to use it as a focal point by performing a grape juice meditation to clear your mind, help solve a problem, or access your creativity and spirituality.

Why grape juice? To aid your meditation, here's the skinny on grapes. Grapes have been cultivated for eight thousand years, which makes them the oldest and probably most widely farmed fruit worldwide. Types include those grown for eating (table grapes), for producing wine, and for making raisins. All grapes contain vitamins A, B, C, K, calcium, iron, manganese, and zinc, so remember their health benefits when you drink your juice.

Grapes symbolize the blessed Eucharist in Christianity, and the juice is drunk during communion as the blood of Christ. Vodou practitioners swear that the smell of grapes draws money and popularity and shrugs off curses. Like most fruit, grapes are an ingredient of potions for fertility and to prompt visions of the future. Grape juice is a favorite substitute for alcoholic libations at holidays and other celebratory events.

Grapes also stand for charity. This fruit was sacred to Dionysus in ancient Greece and to Bacchus in Rome. In fact, cults flourished to these gods, who symbolized inspiration. By analogy, grape juice can be drunk today to gain insights and strengthen the mind. Because they grow in clusters, this fruit brings people with different opinions into unity.

For this meditation, you'll need two lilac-colored or yellow tapers, two candleholders, and a stick of fruit-scented incense. Grape scented is best, but it's hard to find, so any fruity flavor will do. Include an incense burner and matches. For the juice, you want a light-colored liquid—no murky purple—so fill a clear glass with white grape juice.

Place the glass of juice in front of you on the kitchen table with the candles on either side of it. Put the incense burner in a convenient spot where you don't have to inhale the smoke directly. Light the tapers and incense.

Now take a comfortable seat in an upright chair in front of the glass and fix your gaze on it. Immerse your thoughts in the clear citrine-colored liquid. Imagine the wetness and freshness of the juice covering you like water from a pristine sea. Don't drink yet, but mentally savor the sweetness. Visualize yourself skimming across the ocean as easily as a porpoise.

Presently you arrive at a faraway sandy shore. You climb out of the water, shake the droplets off your back, and ascend stone steps to what looks like a Chinese pagoda or temple overlooking the sea. The temple floor is made of cool marble and the pillars that rise to the roof with its upturned corners are of intricately carved wood. Enormous green plants with sun-dappled leaves abound everywhere, and you hear the music of birds warbling in the foliage.

Suddenly you notice an ancient wise man with a long white beard sitting cross-legged on the temple floor. He motions for you to sit beside him, and plush red and gold pillows miraculously appear. You take a seat next to the venerable sage and ask him to guide you on the path to inner knowledge. Listen to his message.

After a few minutes' communion with the revered elder, thank him for his learned counsel. Then turn and skip down the steps back to the ocean, where you glide home.

Slowly float up into your kitchen as if emerging from a deep pool. Ta-da! You're back at your kitchen table once more. Drink the juice now to ground and refresh yourself. Write any messages you received in your journal.

Liquid Recipes to Nourish
Body, Soul, and Journaling

Speaking of journaling, in this section you'll find a set of recipes for liquid refreshments designed to enhance creativity and inspiration for journaling, intuition, concentration, and meditation. The recipes have been engineered to help imbue you with feelings of fulfillment, well-being, and tranquility so you can relax and feel perfectly at ease in your kitchen sanctuary. If we truly are what we eat, perhaps these formulas will also help you select your topics, no matter where or when you decide to do your writing. At the very least, you'll have rustled up a nutritious, delicious treat.

Pear and Apple Cocktail

Here's a simple recipe you can stir up in two minutes. Pears symbolize happiness, comfort, and hope. Apples stand for wisdom, poetry, tranquility, and happiness. They are alleged to help you contact your guardian angel. Lemon balm is for communications and public speaking, and cloves are reputed to bring comfort and solace.

Place the following ingredients in a large glass:

½ cup pear juice
½ cup apple juice (the organic
   kind that is not clear)
⅛ teaspoon lemon balm
Pinch of ground cloves

Stir with a cinnamon stick (to facilitate communications) and add ice if you wish. Sit back and savor the tanginess while you mentally organize the topic you are going to write about.

OOLONG AND LAVENDER TEA

Both oolong tea and lavender leaves and flowers help with grounding and centering. Whereas green tea is either not fermented or only slightly fermented, and black tea is completely fermented, oolong is partially fermented. Its smooth taste is the gourmet's choice. Studies show that oolong is especially beneficial for neurological health, as it aids memory and improves focus. This tea is loaded with antioxidants to help fight infection and detoxify the body. Lavender is a tonic for the central nervous system; it helps reduce stress, combats depression and exhaustion, and heightens awareness.

Boil a cupful of pure spring water. So you don't scorch the botanicals, let the water cool for two minutes before adding the following:

> 1 oolong teabag
> ¼ teaspoon lavender leaves and flowers, fresh
> or dried, in a small muslin bag or tea ball

Let the mixture stand for three minutes; remove the botanicals. Now go to your sanctuary, sip the tea, and prepare to meditate.

LEEK AND POTATO SOUP

This ultimate comfort soup is also an aid for grounding and centering. I like to cook up a potful after the holidays are over to help me regain my focus and peace of mind.

*Before dicing the leeks, you will need to take some care
cleaning them, as bits of dirt and sand tend to get caught
inside the layers. Wash thoroughly and cut off the bottom
of the root and the darkest green leaves on top. Then cut
each leek lengthwise and thoroughly clean out all the dirt
and grit. Potatoes are for fulfillment and grounding; leeks
are for clear-headedness. Carrots are for good luck, garlic
clears the mind and encourages good judgment, parsley is
for strength and courage, and bay leaf is for success.*

$\frac{1}{4}$ cup butter or butter substitute
4 leeks, diced
2 cloves fresh garlic, minced
4 cups organic Yukon potatoes, peeled and diced
2 carrots, peeled and diced
6 cups chicken or vegetable stock
$\frac{1}{4}$ cup fresh parsley, chopped
1 bay leaf
2 cups heavy cream or milk
Salt and pepper to taste
Fresh parsley or thyme for garnish (optional)

Melt the butter in a pan. Add the leeks and garlic and cook
until almost caramelized. Remove the ingredients to a
large pot and add potatoes, carrots, stock, parsley, and bay
leaf. Cook until the potatoes and carrots are soft. Remove
the bay leaf. Cool the mixture (approximately ten minutes) until you can place it in a blender. Blend on high,
adding the cream or milk a little at a time until you get
a creamy consistency. Put the soup back into the pot and
reheat, adding salt and black pepper to taste. If you wish,
garnish with fresh parsley or thyme.

SHAKE UP CREATIVITY SMOOTHIE

This smoothie is designed to enhance your intuition and creativity, both of which help you resonate with your inner being and aid your journaling. Vanilla fosters harmony; coconut confers strength and enhances creativity. Pineapples stand for perfection. Tangerines symbolize inspiration and zest. Bananas lend energy to your creative endeavors, and rose petals are for harmony and balance.

½ pint vanilla ice cream
¼ cup shredded coconut
1 cup canned crushed pineapple
½ cup light cream
3 ounces frozen tangerine juice
 (half of a 6-ounce can—save
 the rest to make juice to add a
 little gusto to your life)
1 small banana
½ cup ice cubes
Toasted shredded coconut and
 fresh rose petals (optional)

Process all the ingredients in a blender until smooth. If you wish, garnish with toasted shredded coconut and a couple of fresh rose petals.

VEGAN STRAWBERRY SMOOTHIE

For a vegan alternative that will equally help develop your intuition, facilitate journaling, and inspire you, follow this recipe whipped up by my vegan friend Nancy Downie. Besides strawberries' health benefits, eating this tasty fruit is alleged to enable a person to see fairies and "the little people." Almonds are for wisdom; in the Afro-Brazilian pantheon, almonds forge a link to the creator god. Ginger spices up creativity, and lemon balm enhances communications.

  1 cup strawberries
  1 small banana, frozen
  2 teaspoons chia seeds
  ½ cup vegan vanilla cashew ice cream
  ½ teaspoon almond extract
  3–4 ice cubes (optional; if you prefer to skip
      the ice cubes, add 1 tablespoon almond
      milk to thin the mixture slightly)
  1 pinch ground ginger
  1 pinch fresh lemon balm or
      ½ capsule lemon balm herb

Liquefy all ingredients in a blender, pour into a tall glass, and sip in your kitchen sanctuary or wherever you write and create.

eight

Other Inner Sanctums

Regretfully, we have to leave this scene of high indulgence in wisdom and haute cuisine to move on to other indoor sanctuaries that you might not have thought could encompass a haven. Later, I'll talk about ways to psychologically protect your threshold.

Perhaps your living space is limited or it's really not convenient to create a hallowed space in your bedroom, bathroom, or kitchen. Whatever the reason, you might consider other rooms, such as a bedroom converted into a home office or even your living room.

Home Offices

Nowadays, many people find it convenient to telecommute from home or even establish their businesses there. While family and friends may feel free to poke around most of the rest of the house, they usually stop short at the home office because they feel uncomfortable encroaching on this sacrosanct zone. You can probably convert this room into a haven where you won't be disturbed without suffering too many repercussions. There are many points to consider when transforming a space such as a spare bedroom into a home office. Following are examples of what three people have done to personalize their home office spaces. Perhaps their ideas will resonate with you and you'll incorporate some into your own office space.

Jennifer's Sun Porch

Jennifer is a certified public accountant whose business is located in a converted sun porch at her home. She chose this room because she claims she's a solar-powered kind of gal who needs plenty of light to pore over all those numbers without losing her concentration. The quality of the light is important to Jennifer, so she has painted the walls a creamy yellow shade and sanded down the hardwood floors to provide contrast. She's acquired an old yellow pine desk with plenty of drawers to keep papers and office supplies organized and out of sight. Jennifer did the remodeling herself because she believes the effort she puts in helps make the space her own. She keeps her office fairly sparse so she's not distracted. The only exception she made was to build shelves in front of the windows where she displays an array of succulents. The plants are easy to care for, love the light, and she finds they add life to a room that otherwise might look too stark.

Jennifer admits that an accountant's lair can sometimes be a seriously dull place. To keep her motivated, she added a touch of humor by pinning to the wall above her desk a photo of ducklings lined up behind their mother. Under the photo she's written "Time to go for a waddle" to remind her to exercise.

TAKEAWAYS FROM JENNIFER'S HOME OFFICE HAVEN: *Keep the room simple and well-lighted to avoid diversions. Put your own energy into its creation, even if you don't strip wood and paint. Include something living and vibrant as well as a touch of humor to generate balance. When designing your home office, will any of these ideas appeal to you?*

Riccardo's Hideaway

Riccardo is an Italian professor at a local university. His home office, a converted den with a fireplace, reflects his passionate intellectual interests and travels. Rather than letting this room evolve, he established the den in less than three days because he needed to have his office functional right away.

Although he probably wouldn't use this term to describe it, Riccardo turned the rough wood mantle over the stone fireplace into a kind of altar that mirrors his fascination with Italian culture. Above the mantle, as a centerpiece, an eighteenth-century Italian costume-ball mask of a ram worked in rich brownish-red leather stares boldly from the wall to the door at anyone who dares cross the threshold. On top of the mantle, under the mask, he's arranged souvenirs collected abroad as well as gifts and legacies having to do with Italy. When he gazes at these things, Riccardo feels surrounded by the love of his Italian friends and family.

Although he enjoys contemplating his mementos, Riccardo has created a purposeful physical separation from them. His desk faces the wall opposite the fireplace, where he's located a relaxation area by placing an overstuffed suede chair and matching brown sofa. This division makes his home office conducive to productivity as well as rest. On a winter's day, he often relaxes on the couch while listening to his favorite Italian operas. Sometimes, he admits, he catches forty winks there, too. When it's time to get to work, he turns his back on the beauty so he doesn't get distracted.

Riccardo's haven also reflects his love of books. One wall is lined from floor to ceiling with them. He explains, "The sight and smell of my books comfort me but also fire my imagination and encourage me to work. Plus it's convenient to have everything I need to consult in one place. If I had to hunt all over the house, I'd waste too much time."

TAKEAWAYS FROM RICCARDO'S OFFICE: *If necessary, you can put together a home office almost instantaneously. By purposefully placing furniture, you can create two areas in one room with separate functions. Mementos having to do with both your work and travels can inspire and comfort you. And don't forget to keep all the items you need for work there for convenience's sake. What kind of mementos might you place in your home office? Will you include some sort of sound system?*

Sierra's Yoga Studio

Perhaps your job doesn't require a home office, but you may still bring home occasional work as well as enjoy pursuing other interests in your sanctuary. Sierra creates dioramas for a nature and science museum and is a yoga enthusiast and rock collector. Since she doesn't have a separate room for a home office, she's established a space in her living room to practice yoga, meditate, and display rocks and gems she's collected.

Because yoga is an Asian practice, she's included representations of the five Chinese elements to help balance her body's chakras and enable her to work efficiently. The plants and gemstones displayed on a couple of low tables symbolize earth. The desk where she works stands for the wood element. For water, she's set a brass cauldron on a stand and fills it with fresh spring water every day for inspiration. The fire element is represented by the votive she keeps burning by the front door. Wind, associated with air, comes from the chime hung outside the door by the front window. She still doesn't know what will represent the metal element but is certain something appropriate will find its way to her. Unlike Riccardo, she considers her living room/studio a work in progress.

When I asked if she minds that her sanctuary is the first room a person sees on entering her home, she replied, "This room is meant to be harmonious and all-embracing. If visitors feel welcome, the conversations that take place here will be stimulating and enjoyable, and further energize the room."

Takeaways from Sierra's yoga studio: *Her last comments suggest that boundaries are important both for what they exclude and include. The point at which boundaries meet can vitalize a space, whether it's a kitchen, home office, or yoga studio, and may even produce new ways of looking at the world. Have you considered how you'll define the boundaries of your home office? You may also want to think about how to incorporate the feng shui principles outlined in chapter 3 to make it a secure, productive, and pleasant environment. And you don't need to establish this haven in an instant: wait for inspiration on some things.*

A Living Room Shelf Shrine

In the last vignette, you read how one woman didn't object to locating her office in her living room; in fact, she took advantage of this more public place to thrive on the energy it brought. Even though the living room is usually a communal area, like Sierra, you can carve out a personal space here. In contemporary times, many homeowners, especially those moving into small houses, have requested that builders construct living room shelves to accommodate more storage space. Also, some people are getting tired of staring at harshly bright white or depressingly gray walls and want to add decorative elements that built-in shelves provide.

Whether it's fitted or consists of a free-standing book case, you can make a mini sanctuary on your living room shelf that reflects your spiritual orientation, philosophy of life, ethnic background, or where you grew up. As you read the next story, contemplate how you might incorporate colors and decorations from your own heritage into your shelf shrine.

In Russia, the color red is very significant. In fact, the words "red" and "beautiful" are synonymous. So Red Square and the Red Army, at least in Russian, are both beautiful. To celebrate her cultural heritage, Tatiana has collected Russian crafts colored predominantly in red. She's arranged an attractive display of pottery, painted spoons, dolls, and embroidered cloths on her living room shelf. Her goal is to find something in every known shade of red. On entering her living room, I was wowed by the elaborate tableau, which, as often happens with visitors, led to a discussion of Russian traditions and culture.

Do you know of any significant colors from your heritage? What kind of objects speak to you of your own childhood and background? Perhaps it's a toy cast-iron stove that represents what your great-grandmother used to cook on or a model of the blue Beetle your granddad once drove to take the family to the circus. Would you place that kind of memento on a shelf shrine or would you highlight something else?

Threshold Protection

It's no secret that the world's population is mushrooming and that more and more people are flocking to our already overcrowded cities. Even the suburbs are not immune to congestion, as houses constructed in new developments are creeping closer together. And with the increasing number of condominiums being built, it's not unusual for homeowners to share at least one wall—not to mention the new phenomenon of dividing a previous one-house lot in two so a house-behind-a-house can be erected. With more cars, pedestrians, and bikes flooding our streets, it's no wonder people feel anxious to establish firm boundaries between their homes and the outside world to protect their privacy. This situation exists even in cultures accustomed to communal living and dwelling in close proximity.

People in other parts of the world have created unique ways to erect a boundary between their homes and the outside world, starting with their thresholds. The threshold has long been respected as the resident's hallowed precinct. So ingrained is this idea in our psyches that even in horror fiction, a vampire can't enter a dwelling unless the occupant extends an invitation. Here are some customs not specifically related to protection but which allude to the importance of thresholds in cultures worldwide.

Doormats in Britain

If you visit anyone in Britain, you will inevitably find a bristly doormat outside the resident's front door, even if the dwelling is a high-rise apartment. Whether it's raining cats and dogs or the sun has shone for a week, all visitors automatically pause before crossing the threshold and vigorously wipe their shoes on the mat. Perhaps this habit represents an awareness, albeit unconscious, that the occupant's home is truly an inner sanctum.

First Footing in Scotland

The image of feet on thresholds reminds me of a delightful Scottish and Irish custom called "first footing." The first person who steps over the threshold after midnight on New Year's Day is supposed to foretell the kind of luck the household will experience throughout the year. If the visitor has dark hair, the luck will be good. This superstition harkens back to the days of Viking raids. The one person you didn't want to see at your door was a blond Norseman decked out in a horned helmet and with an upraised sword in hand, hellbent on pillage and destruction.

At one New Year's Eve celebration (the Scots call it Hogmanay) that I attended in Scotland, around thirty of us were dancing Scottish flings in the great hall of a country home when a loud rap on the front door immediately silenced us all. The homeowner let in a mysterious fellow who made for the hearth toting a large canvas bag, from which he extracted a lump of coal, a handful of fragrant herbs, and a pinch of salt, all of which he threw on the blazing fire. This raven-haired gentleman also had kisses for the ladies.

The homeowner invited the man to join in the festivities, and we all continued to dance lively Highland reels, consume holiday delicacies, and imbibe more than one wee dram of fine whiskey. After a while, the first-footer went on his way, with a gift bottle of malt in his bag, to visit the next home, and so on, until dawn, which breaks late in the winter up north. Looking back on that sparkling evening, I believe that the luckiest person in the room was the first-footer, who brought us joy and, in return, received gifts, thanks, and many kisses!

Carrying the Bride

Nobody knows for sure the origin of the custom where the groom lifts the bride across the threshold to their home, but it certainly carries a lot of weight in many cultures worldwide. The reason may once have been to keep at bay the monsters and spiteful elves that lurk beneath everyone's threshold (didn't you know?), just waiting for their chance to strike. Or perhaps the groom, being a superstitious sort, worried that his bride would stumble through the doorway in her dainty slippers (or high heels) and portend bad luck for their marriage. No matter the source, couples all over the world have been inspired to adopt this sweet custom.

In spite of not believing in silly superstitions, my husband followed tradition and picked me up and carried me over our threshold (with me clutching the champagne and basket of strawberries). Such a romantic experience! For me, being lifted over the threshold beautifully and ceremonially marked my transition from single woman to married life. What a way to begin looking forward to future experiences together!

Chinese Door Guardians

Door guardians play an important role in Chinese mythology. In former times, over their front gates and thresholds, people would mount images of these defensive gods carved from red-colored peach wood in the belief that they drove off ghosts, wild beasts, and human intruders. Nowadays people are less concerned with phantoms and mythological creatures, and instead have adapted this custom to improving quality of life.

Gone are the peach wood door guardians, replaced by red paper banners painted with protection symbols (the color red is for both protection and good luck). At the New Year's festival, some householders express both their wishes for prosperity and their literary creativity by writing their desires on the banners in the form of couplets. Others communicate their political point of view or philosophy of life.

Celtic Hole Stones

On the other side of the world, the ancient Celts of the British Isles were fascinated by stones with natural holes in them, which they named "luck stones" (*an cloc cosanta*). As the region Christianized, these rocks became known as "witch stones," "hag stones," and "holey stones." Some of the rocks found in archeological digs are small enough to be strung on necklaces as talismans, presumably to increase the wearer's personal power and enhance their psychic abilities. Megalith hole stones can still be seen near the thresholds of stone circles. Archeologists posit that their purpose was to protect, heal, and consecrate marriages by passing the couple through the hole. After death, corpses were also carried through the hole to ease the soul's journey to the world beyond.

New World Methods

Threshold protection customs also thrive in the Western Hemisphere. For example, Mexicans keep pots of aloe vera plants near the front door to absorb negativity that might try to ooze into the home. Haitians do the same thing with glasses full of sugarcane rum. Adherents of African-American Vodou place burned-out light bulbs in a basket at the front door to reflect harmful thoughts back to the perpetrator. These practitioners also believe that the bulbs will light up on a higher spiritual plane and discharge the negative vibrations there.

Here in the Southwest, some Native Americans keep a bowlful of colorful turquoise by the front door, a pink conch shell, red coral, or a few eagle feathers to ward off negativity. Modern-day Peruvian Indians hang the season's last dried stalk and ear of corn over the doorway to invite the protection of the Corn Goddess.

Mezuzahs

In many Jewish homes, a case called a mezuzah is affixed to the right side of the doorpost as a declaration of devotion and to protect the home. Inside the small, narrow case, a tiny parchment scroll is meticulously handwritten in special writing with a command from the biblical book of Deuteronomy for the occupants to keep God's word in head and heart. On the back of the scroll, the first letter of one of the names of God is written in Hebrew. The relic is nailed at an angle because the rabbis couldn't agree on whether it should be affixed horizontally or vertically, so they compromised!

The materials from which mezuzahs are made are incredibly beautiful and quite diverse, including wood, metal, silver filigree, copper, pewter, bronze, brass, and more. Mezuzahs are recognized as true works of art, and many are highly collectible.

Protecting Your Own Threshold

I'm not suggesting that you adopt a mezuzah or any of the religious customs I've mentioned unless, of course, you are of that heritage. But if a video cam aimed at your front porch isn't enough to satisfy you, there are several things you can do to physically protect your threshold. First, explore your own background and heritage. Ask an elderly relative about what they remember their grandparents doing to protect the household, or take one of those mail-in DNA tests to find out about your roots. Then begin searching for the measures your ancestors took to provide protection for their homes. If you still come up short, following are some general suggestions you can choose to work with, depending on your inclinations. None of these ideas depend on any specific religious or ethnic orientation; all are in the public domain.

Botanical Amulets and Talismans

Throughout history certain botanicals have been ascribed protective powers, probably because before the advent of modern medicine, people relied on them to cure illness and disease. The defensive value of botanicals largely depends on belief. If you're confident that burying a bagful of sage and salt under your front porch or hanging a sprig of dried basil over the door frame will deflect negativity, it might do that. If you're not a believer, though, the gesture probably won't work.

Spicy, strong-flavored herbs like ground cayenne pepper and mustard seed are alleged to act as shields, just like basil and sage do. A more practical use for cayenne and mustard seed is to sprinkle a line of one of the powdered herbs across a window ledge or on the doorway floor to discourage ants and other pests from invading. However, I don't recommend this measure for households with pets as the herbs may be distasteful to them or even harmful when your furry friends lick their paws. (My housecleaner has suggested that salt works just as well, and she should know!) Salt is also thought to absorb negativity.

For a less messy and certainly more attractive solution, you might want to plant various protection botanicals around the front of your house or grow them in pots on the porch. These include bamboo, ferns, juniper, lilies, and marigolds. You can also plant the feverfew herb, which has the added benefit of chasing off flies.

For apartment dwellers, a sachet bag filled with any five of the following protection botanicals will accomplish the same task: angelica, basil, bay, cinnamon, cinquefoil, dill, frankincense, lavender, marigold flowers, mint, mountain ash berries, rue, sage. Dry the herbs before inserting them in the bag so they don't grow mold. Tie the opening shut with a red satin ribbon and hang the bag over your doorway (the red ribbon is for protection). The herbs will protect and freshen the front portion of your home with their light herbal fragrance and create a congenial ambience. I don't recommend garlic bulbs, though. You don't want the odor to scare off your friends along with your enemies—unless your enemies are vampires!

Bury a Talisman for Good Luck

Earlier I mentioned the tradition of carrying the bride through the doorway and how it may have originated in the belief that something evil lurked beneath the threshold. In the same vein, some people bury items by their doors because they have faith in the protective value of these objects. Any of the abovementioned botanicals will help defend the home. Some people also hold that certain objects will draw good luck. Popular items to bury that are alleged to attract good fortune include two crossed needles or five new pennies. If you want to spend some money, bury a lucky gemstone, like tiger's eye, or a black tourmaline to repel negativity. Don't forget to disinter the gem and take it with you when you move! It is said that burying food under your front porch will ensure that you'll never go hungry. If you try this last method, my advice is to bury the food deep so the raccoons and other critters won't get into it.

Witch Balls

One of the prettier-looking ways said to protect your threshold from bad vibes and evildoers is to suspend a witch ball from the doorway or place it in front of a window where the light will shine on it. Witch balls are silvery glass orbs somewhat larger than the typical Christmas tree ball ornament. Originally, these ornaments had nothing to do with witches. They first appeared during the seventeenth century in Bohemia, a region famous for its glassblowers. Around Christmastime, the blowers would congregate in beer halls and pubs to enjoy some holiday cheer. After quaffing tankards of ale, they'd compete to see who could blow the largest bubble before it broke.

Their clever wives, recognizing a goldmine when they saw one, gathered the unbroken balls. They swished a silver nitrate solution around the inside of the ornaments to give them a silvery sheen and sold them at the local Christmas bazaars as threshold decorations. Later, balls were exported to England and America, where they became associated with the holly boughs people hung over their doors to keep evil at bay.

Today, lovely examples of witch balls can be found in New England antique shops. Ironically, many storekeepers refuse to part with them because they believe their good luck will walk out the door with the witch ball. If you manage to separate a shop owner from a ball, it will be well worth the price. Whether or not you believe in the ball's power to banish evil, it will make a captivating addition to your door decor—more enchanting than an old iron horseshoe!

nine

Simplifying Your Space and Your Life

In this chapter, we take up another way to refine your sacred space—by decluttering and simplifying it.

I imagine many readers have at least heard of the television programs *Hoarding: Buried Alive* on TLC and *Hoarders* on A&E. You may be puzzled by how some people could let their homes deteriorate so utterly. Those shows present extreme examples of what overconsumption can amount to in our consumer-oriented society. Few of us are completely immune to the hoarding instinct. UCLA's Center on Everyday Lives of Families conducted an eye-opening study on middle-class homes in Los Angeles. The results are printed in the book *Life at Home in the Twenty-First Century: 32 Families Open Their Doors.*

Researchers who interviewed participants found when working moms arrive home after an exhausting day, their stress levels, already high, shoot up dramatically as they view with horror the creeping invasion of clutter choking them. Dad and the kids are almost equally affected. Despite people's urge to clean up, fully one quarter of their garages become so packed with stuff that they can no longer park a car there, so they resign themselves to trolling for street parking.

Where does this obsession to accumulate originate? In part, it's a holdover from the fifties through the eighties, when folks competed to "keep up with the Joneses." The highest mark of status and success was defined by what and how much a person possessed. The series *Mad Men* portrays with dark humor these preoccupations in our society during those times. *The Americans* series reveals this phenomenon on a much darker scale.

To help push Americans down that slippery slope, around thirty years ago stuff suddenly got less expensive. Blame it, if you dare, on low-priced imports from China and other Asian nations. Clothing, linens, toys, tools, home gadgets, electronics, and personal care products became ridiculously affordable. New big-box stores hawking discounted merchandise, often in quantity, proliferated in this country, and the average shopper lined up to take advantage of the bargains. Advertisers bombarded us—and still do—with exhortations to "buy now or lose out on the deal." No longer finding door-to-door sales profitable, they assault us on television, phone, and the internet. Besides, we are constantly being reminded by those in power that growth is good for the economy, and part of growth is consumption. Many people still boast about ours being a consumer-oriented society.

Current Trend Toward Simplification

Lately, consumerism has begun to shift into a new phase. As imported goods get less expensive, quality deteriorates. Eventually, many so-called bargains lose status. At approximately the same time, a change begins taking place in where people choose to live. Rather than getting stuck with a big house and garden in the suburbs along with the accompanying maintenance issues, young people in particular are opting to live in apartments and condos near where they work and play. The attraction of a city center where a vibrant, busy, nonstop life can be enjoyed draws them like bees to honey. Moreover, baby boomers are downsizing from their large family homes to more manageable city apartments or retirement communities where facilities are convenient and available to them and where they can more easily make friends their own age. To accomplish these changes, they become determined to rid themselves of excess. Their middle-aged children either receive many of these things as gifts or inheritances, and they, too, become anxious to divest themselves of the overflow.

Cashing in on, or perhaps even helping to generate this fresh outlook, are a plethora of decluttering gurus, many of whom have written how-to books on the subject. Chief among these volumes are *The Life-Changing Magic of Tidying Up: The Japanese Art of Decluttering and Organizing* by Marie Kondo, *Lighten Up* by Peter Walsh, *Unclutter Your Life in One Week* by Erin Rooney Doland, *Minimalism: Live a Meaningful Life* by Joshua Fields Millburn and Ryan Nicodemus, *Stuffocation* by James Wallman, and others.

These books hold a special appeal for millennials because they emphasize freedom, especially freedom from responsibilities, and the value of experiences over things as keys to true happiness. In these authors' worldviews, things make you happy for only a short time. As you get used to them being around, you no longer value them highly; in fact, you tend to forget them. On the other hand, these experts emphasize that experiences such as that eco-trip up the Amazon or mountain-climbing expedition in the Himalayas will forge an everlasting memory. Moreover, you can connect with others through these shared experiences, which is something you can't do with things. Instead of comparing iPhone models, you can compare your respective trips to Anguilla.

Young people still buy low-cost material goods such as lightweight and disposable merchandise from Target or IKEA—things they can let go of easily without forming any attachments. They often reject what came from the past— the precious possessions handed down for generations such as china, crystal, silver, and great grandad's cuckoo clock— simply because they don't value history as much.

Whether these self-described simplification authorities and their philosophical notions should be followed unreservedly is a matter of debate, and one I will return to at the end of this chapter. For now, let's assume we could all use some simplification in our lives to make us feel happier and less stressed. In this chapter I will suggest some ways to declutter. Many of my tips are based on personal experience from having to divest myself of my parents' and in-law's estates, and more recently from my ongoing efforts to downsize my own home. Because so many books have been written on this subject, I only cover the bare bones here.

Tackling the Clutter

As the abundance of books on the market indicate, there are many ways to attack the clutter in your home and successfully downsize. From more than one source, I've read that you should hold each object in your hand and, as you look at it, ask yourself, "Does this object spark joy?" I'd rather ask myself, "Does this object stimulate a memory that moves me so much I want to keep it around as a reminder of my past?" Every item you hold will trigger some memory; the question is, is it special?

Here are some other ideas. Try to curb spending on new acquisitions. Do you need that slickly advertised set of mango knives you'll probably only use once and which won't do anything but peel mangos? Do you really want to waste twenty dollars on a widget that will sell at next summer's yard sale for a buck? Do you already possess an identical or very similar item? Then one must go. If you're moving to a new abode, it's best to focus on the space. Rather than thinking about how to squeeze what you have into another space, visualize what exactly you want it to look like. Eliminate anything that doesn't fit your vision.

The Worst Offenders

I advise paying special attention to some of the worst offenders when it comes to unnecessary accumulation. Take clothes, for example. Some decluttering gurus will tell you that if you haven't worn an item in a year, you should sell or donate it. Personally, I have fashionable clothes in my wardrobe that I haven't worn for a few years. A couple still have their price tags on them! I know that at the right time and place, I will wear some garments again because they look good on me. I agree you should donate outdated clothing or things that no longer fit. On the other hand, my mother kept a few different clothing sizes in her closet because her weight was always changing. She held back only the best, nicest, most expensive outfits to give herself a treat when at last she could fit into them. People often commented on what a snazzy dresser she was. While you're at it, return those extra hangers to the dry cleaner. They'll love you for it.

Books comprise another category of offender, and—full disclosure—I admit I'm guilty when it comes to hoarding books. I don't seem to be able to consign these old friends— and I do consider them friends—to the donation box. Decluttering experts recommend relying on e-books to indulge your book fix, but sometimes I want to hold a physical book, feel the weight of the pages, and inhale the dry fragrance of a venerable volume. So this is what I've done.

First, I glanced at the literally thousands of books our family possesses. I eliminated doubles, triples, and even a few quadruples, keeping only the best volumes. I took some classics, including children's books I would never reread, and sold them. (More on selling shortly.) I also jettisoned to the library piles of books from my former academic career, keeping only old favorites. Then I tackled my favorite genre, which happens to be mysteries. I retained only the few volumes and authors I think one day I may return to. On a separate shelf (okay, two shelves), I placed all the mysteries I've bought but haven't yet had a chance to read. Systematically, I'm wending my way through those, and once I finish a book, it goes into the donation box or a Little Free Library. My husband is doing the same thing with his favorite genre, philosophy. In this way, we've been able to liberate ourselves of at least a thousand books.

An offshoot of books are VHS tapes and board games. Throw away outmoded VHS tapes except those of memorable events such as a wedding. Tapes can be digitalized onto memory disks. As to used CDs, I've found I can sell those to used bookstores along with books. I'm not keen on board games, but decluttering experts recommend you keep only four or five of your favorites and donate the rest.

Office files, like old projects and receipts, can be stored in the Cloud or on Instapaper or Pinterest. Here I recommend a modicum of caution; at the very least, keep paper originals of leases and licenses. Also, I like to retain all paper tax documents for ten years (seven years is the general recommendation, but my CPA says ten, and I believe him). I'm concerned the internet will get hacked or otherwise fail, however briefly, inevitably when I'm suddenly being audited. I also like to keep the original receipts for anything of value I've bought over the years like jewelry, fine furniture, antiques, textiles, etc. Such receipts fit handily into a shoebox. This is my solution; you may do something different.

Outdated electronics, like cell phones and old laptops, and long-abandoned sports equipment represent another area ripe for deep pruning. Get rid of that gym equipment you no longer use. Take it to a sports equipment recycle store, and for heaven's sake, throw away those moldy old plastic water bottles and holey running shoes!

Over time, you may have built up a collection of tools for home and garden or perhaps inherited these implements from different branches of the family. Treat them as you would the kitchen gadgets you've doubled-up on or as one-use items. You don't need eighteen pairs of pliers or six pruning shears, five of which need repair anyway.

Take courage and open your bathroom cabinets and drawers. Eek! Are personal care and bathroom products you'll never use lurking there, slowly outliving their expiration dates? Are your shelves harboring too many hair dryers and old hair accessories? Chuck them out!

Downsizing

Maybe your desire to simplify is linked to downsizing. You may be moving from the suburbs to a smaller place in the city for work or to a smaller home, condo, or senior living facility after retirement. Believe me, I sympathize with your situation and understand the difficult decisions you face. I watched my parents downsize from a very large home with two auxiliary abodes to one smaller home, then to a condo, and eventually to an independent living unit.

When my mother passed away suddenly, she still owned a 2,000-square-foot condo that I needed to empty and repaint in a month because I already had a buyer. At one point, my house, which isn't pint-sized, was so stuffed I couldn't make it to the phone in time to answer when it rang. I also filled the garage, guest house, and pony barn, rented a storage unit, and had items hanging around in the driveway and on the front porch. It's been twelve years and I'm still getting rid of things, mainly because the time has come for me and my husband to downsize to a smaller place too. (I told you I sympathize with your plight!)

So far, I've given some general suggestions. Here are some specifics. Ask yourself if you really want to pay to ship this item to a new dwelling, even if it's only across town. Bear in mind that movers admit that 60 percent of the time, the cost of a move will outweigh the value of the contents. Think books! Auxiliary pots and pans! Heavy tools!

Visualize your new space; take measurements, if needed, and decide how much you want or can have in the space without overcrowding. There are some computer programs out there to help you with this task or you can go old school and use a piece of paper, a ruler, and a pencil. Then line up the items you clearly have too many of. These might include chairs, crystal, more than one or two sets of dishware, end tables (where did they all come from?), extra flatware, an overabundance of framed pictures, single glasses, sets of items you no longer use, purses, kitchen and home gadgets (especially one-use items like the ice cream maker unless this is a hobby), knick-knacks you're no longer interested in, mugs, office supplies, personal care products, quilts, remotes, rugs, shoes, silver, worn out and mismatched linens, and threadbare towels. Whew! Give each item a critical once-over. You don't need to dispose of everything, but what are you willing to live without? In my situation, I inherited twenty-seven antique model ships—lovely to look at dirt magnets that my cats loved to swipe at for amusement. It took me three years to sell them, but finally they're all gone except for the photos I took.

Decluttering specialists talk about "memory clutter." By this, they mean items you're attached to because they evoke certain memories. These whizzes suggest you photograph those items so you can look back fondly and retrieve old memories when yours, perhaps, is failing. I think this ploy works, but only up to a point. It's useful for a whole lot of things to which you are not overly attached. Still, there are some things neither you nor a relative for whom you might be helping to downsize would be happy to walk away from. For example, the dress costume you hand-sewed for your daughter's first school play or the small gilded Victorian pedestal mirror the boy I almost married but didn't gave me when we visited Greek Town in Detroit. Select a few fond memories to keep with you. You might want to limit yourself to a number such as ten or twenty—whatever works for you.

How to Divest Yourself of Excess

For getting rid of what I call "excessibilia," I have three words for you: sell, donate, trash. Don't be afraid to let go of something you may need later. This doesn't happen often, but if it does, you can probably buy new.

Make sure everything you want to keep has a home. Find its home in the new space first before going out and buying all of those cute little storage bins. For me, storing small items in old shoeboxes works well, and I don't have to pay for the box.

Choose a specific time every week, day, or month to work on downsizing so you're less apt to procrastinate. I've read some books that recommend you let go of ten things a day for a year or that after you purge, you should end up with only one hundred possessions. I find such strategies a tad overzealous. The last thing you want to do is make yourself feel ashamed or depressed if you can't live up to somebody else's arbitrary benchmark. Nobody has the right formula for downsizing but you. You decide how much you're comfortable getting rid of. Once you've discarded the item, take it to its destined place, be it a friend, relative, resale store, charity, or, as a last resort, the trash.

Sell

To permanently relieve yourself of clutter, you can sell, donate, or throw away. Think of it as recycling, at least for the first two categories, as the discarded items won't end up in the landfill. If you sell an item, you're also giving yourself a little boost by earning a reward for all your hard work. I get a thrill whenever I make a personal or online sale on Etsy or Facebook Marketplace because I'm linking things I no longer want or need with somebody who really wants and appreciates them. On my Etsy site, I've received scores of positive reviews from people who are delighted with their purchases.

Also, when a customer finds "just the right thing" they've been looking for at one of my yard sales, I rejoice for them. All those vintage items, some of them quite beautiful and full of memories, will take on a second life in another person's home.

Before you're ready to sell, consider the following. What is the minimum price you'll accept for a given item? Sometimes you'll know, but if you don't, I suggest searching for similar merchandise on eBay or other sales sites. If you have some really nice, expensive antiques or classy vintage items, you might get your best price at an auction or an estate liquidation. Beware! Thoroughly vet auction houses, attend auctions held by your prospective choices, and carefully read the fine print before you sign on. When liquidating my mother's estate, I was rushed and had a houseful of things to discard, so I simply did not pay enough attention. I was taken to the cleaners by an auction company that was not very experienced, too expensive, and sold things for a song. My cold comfort is I've since found that many of my friends have had similar experiences. To avoid disappointment, contact the American Society of Appraisers. The appraisers listed are expensive, but they've been vetted, know what they're doing, and will save you a lot in the long run. Plus, they will probably manage to sell most of what they took, as they wisely select what they know will sell well for them.

Another way to price your things is to buy the current year's *Antique Trader Antiques & Collectibles Price Guide*, published by Krause. This will cost you under $20 and is well worth the price. You can borrow the magazine from your local library for free. Document each item and insure anything valuable. If you don't have receipts, find an old photo of the item in those boxes of photos you've inherited.

Many online sites will flog your merchandise for you. A few of the most popular are eBay, Amazon, Craigslist, and Etsy. Some offer the seller better terms than others. For example, you can post free on Craigslist and Facebook Marketplace. Unfortunately, problems sometimes arise between sellers and buyers on those sites when they come face-to-face. One solution is to meet in a very public place and bring along a friend or relative for protection.

Personally, I've had a lot of success with Etsy. Originally created for craftspeople who want to sell online, Etsy also has a vintage section. As of this writing, anything prior to 2000 is considered vintage. Although it costs twenty cents to list an item, Etsy will calculate the shipping for you for free, and you don't pay it: the buyer does. Etsy even adds up your monthly sales for you and provides tax information. You can state on your site that you don't issue refunds, and Etsy usually stands behind the seller in disputes.

One thing I've learned by posting vintage merchandise is that there's a market for just about anything. Although American millennials may eschew delicate crystal, gold-rimmed china, and antique silver, people from other cultures who live in the US still value such refinements. Elaborate dinner parties held for several honored relatives and guests form an integral part of other cultures' hosting and entertaining. And the items don't have to be antiques. I sold a vintage 1950s grain mill and meat grinder still in its original box to a woman who wrote me that her grinder had broken down and she had lost an irreplaceable part. She was overjoyed to find a machine that I surely was never going to use.

Next on your list are consignment shops and thrift stores. Their advantage is that they are usually local, take many items for resale, and have a high merchandise turnover. More customers shop these stores than you could ever manage to draw to a yard sale. Also, the owners/managers often set prices much higher than you'd have the moxie to do. On the downside, they take 50 percent of all sales. (After all, they have a hefty overhead.) Since they need to make quick sales, they can be downright picky about those precious heirlooms you hauled over to their store. Avoid disappointment by visiting these shops often or sending them photos online. See what's selling and only offer what's in demand now. Keep an eagle eye out for when your time's up with an item (usually kept for two or three months) and take it back or the store will donate it and you won't get any of the money.

I suggest you get to know the people working where you intend to sell. Around the holidays, I bring homemade cookies for the staff of my favorite consignment shop, fortuitously called Clutter. I've gotten to know everyone there, and they make a good effort to sell my things for me. I once took in a huge Horchow Chinoiserie grandfather clock that simply would not sell. Knowing it would cost me a packet to dismantle and take it home, the owner decided to keep it on. The clock became a kind of store mascot and sold six months later to an out-of-state doctor.

The final position on your sales list is the inevitable yard sale. Yes, it will cost you time and effort, and you may get rained out (I'd say you have a 70 percent chance of at least some rain or wind; I even suffered through a freak June snowstorm). But you keep all of the profits and, depending on where you live, may not have to pay tax on sales. Plenty of books and websites discuss how to gain the most profit from a yard sale. Here's a mere thimbleful of advice from some-body who conducts yearly sales.

Begin gathering items early. If I'm doing a sale in June, I get started in January. Box up things (and label the boxes) according to where you'll place them on the tables. I have separate tables for books, electronics, tools, linens, kitchen, toys, etc. I make large signs (legible at twenty yards) and attach them to the tables. This is convenient for the shop-per looking for something specific. Each item should be clean and unbroken and displayed artfully on its table. I always cov-er my tables with attractive, solid-colored cloths. (Patterns disguise the merchandise.) I erect a second layer at the back of the table with boards and bricks where I display smaller items up high, so they are noticeable and out of the way of children's roaming fingers. That way, I also get more exhibit room out of each table.

I plug in a long cord near gadgets for potential customers to verify things are in working order. I use the same cord to set up a boom box to play music from a classical or easy listening station. If you sell something broken, such as a piece of electronic equipment, clearly label the item "as is"— that is, needing repair. I don't provide snacks. In my city I would need to have a food preparation license, and candy, cookies, and cupcakes can be sticky and messy. Have plenty of ones, fives, tens, twenties, and change on hand so you don't have to run to the bank.

Finally, advertise, advertise, advertise, at least as much as your budget will allow. Try local newspapers, the free papers you find at the grocery store, Facebook, Craigslist, Garage-Sale Hunter, YardSale Search, and local organizations like Nextdoor and local buy/sell/trade online sites. Make up a few large, very visible signs for the neighborhood to direct people to your house, and remove the signs promptly after the sale is over. You may want to contact a charity to bring a truck to pick up leftovers for donations so you don't have to pack it all up again and store it. You'll also want to document the specific items you're donating for tax purposes.

Donate

Speaking of donations, plenty of charities will take your offerings, including Habitat for Humanity, the Salvation Army, ARC thrift stores, the Humane Society, and Disabled American Veterans. One of my favorites is Goodwill because they take the money they earn and turn it into training programs to prepare disabled employees or those with little educational background for a career. In the past you could take up to $500 worth of donations off your taxes without any fuss. Over that amount, you needed to list every item, price it, and photograph it, too, or risk an audit from the IRS. Unfortunately, under current tax laws, donations must total $14,000 or the same amount totaled over three years for you to be able to take the deduction. Still, I believe that donating is good for the soul and the environment. I think it's prudent to list and price each item even if it isn't necessary. Goodwill and other charities have lists of suggested prices for books, clothing, games, furniture, sports equipment, electronics, etc. The items you donate, although gently used, should be in decent shape—nothing broken, no parts missing.

Go through your clothes before you donate; you never know where forgotten cash or jewelry may be hiding. Before I donated my mother's clothes, I checked each item and came up with over $200.

Trash

As a last resort, you may have to throw away some things. Items in this category include what is stained, torn, or broken and mementos meaningful only to you. In the process of downsizing, I discarded a stack of old newspapers from my middle school days when I wrote articles for the school newspaper and also was an editor. Rereading the papers was bittersweet because it brought up many memories. In the end, they all went into the recycle bin, and I am lighter in body, mind, and spirit.

Musings on Clutter

As you can probably tell, I'm all for decluttering. Every day I try to dispose of something I don't really want or need. However, as with everything in life, one can go overboard. In my opinion, some of these self-described decluttering gurus have done just that. In their enthusiasm for the physical and psychological benefits of simplification, they seem to shame the person whose home is less than perfectly organized as being somehow defective. There must be something terribly wrong with you, they imply, if you have permitted the Great Evil Clutter to overtake your life. After all, they posit, a cluttered home is an indication of a cluttered brain. Dispense with the mess and you will experience tranquility and joy and regain power over your life.

Does anybody really believe that? I don't think divesting myself of all my excess baggage will lead me on the path to discovering my inner beauty and achieving my brilliant mission in life. Sometimes I look at the cold, soulless, oversimplified spaces proudly displayed in home decorating books, television shows, and magazines and wonder if they may actually reveal an overly simple brain. Everybody is different, and some people thrive in complex environments.

Pamela Druckerman wrote "The Clutter Cure," an insightful op-ed for the *New York Times,* on February 17, 2015. Like me, she questioned whether the act of physical decluttering would really make a person happy. She ended her article by writing, "It's consoling to think that, beneath all these distractions, we'll discover our shining, authentic selves, or even achieve a state of 'mindfulness.' But I doubt it. I'm starting to suspect that the joy of ditching all of our stuff is just as illusory as the joy of acquiring it all was. Less may be more, but it's still not enough."

So if you enjoy your collections or want to hang on to things that evoke beautiful memories of a loved one or remind you of a wonderful trip you once took, I advise you to keep them. These things are yours to cherish, and there's no shame in that.

Downsizing is a process. Decluttering is a process. In one sense you will never finish, so don't feel you need to do it all at once. Slow and steady is my mantra. Also, complete each task you do all the way. Don't leave something "for another day" or you'll never finish. As you work, take the bags to the trash or donation center right away. Don't let things pile up. If you do, there's always the danger you or somebody in your family will want to retrieve items they previously signed off on. ("But that was my favorite shirt!" my husband moans.) And don't get discouraged if the results don't look perfect. As some things vacate the premises, others tend to fly in and take their place.

In the next chapter, I'll expand, so to speak, on the topic of downsizing by discussing some of the adjustments you may need to make after moving to a less complex environment.

ten

Celebrating Small Spaces

Congratulations! You've managed to declutter, downsize, and move to simpler digs with less square footage. Now you may be asking yourself how in the world you will transform this reduced space into a haven you can love as much as your former home. In this chapter, I'll offer tips on how to organize and personalize a small apartment or condo. Then I'll discuss two even smaller spaces: dorm and hospital rooms. Finally, I'll touch on tiny homes. Many of the tips given in one section apply to all.

Apartments and Condos

In your downsizing efforts, you've probably sold off a ton of furniture. Here's one way to spend some of your proceeds wisely. The first rule small apartment decorator experts insist you must abide by is functionality. Every stick of furniture must have a useful reason for being there or it's a waste of precious floor space. To comply with this dictum, you may want to invest in a few multipurpose items such as a hollow ottoman that doubles as a storage bin or a drop-leaf table you can open when hosting dinner guests. Ingenious dining tables that swing out from under countertops can also be had. In the past, Murphy beds that drop down from inside a wall have gotten a bad rap as being lumpy and uncomfortable, but these types of beds have evolved with the times. Why not visit a demo store and try different styles to see what you think? A cozy day bed provides another intelligent option. Day beds are designed to fit flush against a wall, and if you add plenty of sumptuous throw pillows, the bed can double as a sofa.

While simplification gurus are all for function first, they caution not to sacrifice personal expression—that is, style. One former prison inmate I know tells me of another inmate who, on being released, rented a small apartment. The walls were painted institutional white, and the light hanging from the living room ceiling was white metal, exactly like the overhead in his erstwhile abode. With his landlord's permission, the first thing he did was upgrade to a candelabra-style fixture. Then he repainted the walls a warm, vibrant sunshine yellow.

Walls are one area where you can let your individuality run wild. Are they painted the way you like? If not, and if you're in an apartment situation and your landlord allows it, repaint. Light colors will brighten and make the space appear larger than it is, but those hues can be boring. To break up the monotony, use two lighter colors and one darker accent color either for a wall, pillows, rugs, or painted furniture.

Don't pile on too many different hues or the space will shrink and look chaotic.

If your landlord doesn't allow you to paint your apartment, or even if you're in your own condo, you can add color in other ways. Vivid area rugs, multi-hued throw pillows, and a richly colored bedspread, with all of these things in coordinating colors, will animate monochromatic walls and carpet. Get creative about what you hang on the walls, too. An intriguing tapestry, imaginative painting, or posters of faraway travel destinations, flowers, landscapes, or favorite musical groups will go a long way toward personalizing your space.

Now that your walls are fresh and gleaming, you can return to the challenge of functionality. One idea is to take advantage of vertical space for storage. Attach a book case to a wall. Fill it with books, but don't compact too much. You want to leave room for framed photos, a few knickknacks, a favorite vase, and other cherished memorabilia you couldn't bring yourself to jettison during your purge. Backs of closet doors also afford opportunities to hang a belt, blouse, skirt, or shoe storage rack. One source suggests using the pockets of an over-the-door shoe organizer to store cleaning products, small office supplies, or kitchen spices.

Plants make a lovely living addition to indoor vertical landscaping. Visualize how elegant a living wall of potted plants on vertical storage racks might look. Indoor greenery also helps remove carbon dioxide and other toxins from the air and adds oxygen. Plants can become a rewarding substitute for the outdoor garden you used to tend. You may want to select ones that require little water, and some that aren't fussy about lighting, especially if you expect to do a lot of traveling. A superior choice is the peace lily (*Spathiphyllum* sp.), which can go into a windowless bathroom. The lily's gentle white flowers will remove toxic chemicals from the air like acetone, benzene, and formaldehyde.

Although cacti need to go in a sunny window, they require very little water or care. If you're not enamored of cactus prickles, choose the light succulent paddle plant, another sun lover that can make do with little water, or an air plant that requires practically no water. The aloe vera (*Aloe barbadensis*) likes moderate light four hours per day but only needs to be watered every week or two. A Norfolk Island pine (*Araucaria heterophylla*), yet another easy plant to grow, will create a positive flow of chi in a stark corner. Be careful, though, as this tree grows two feet per year on the average and up to two hundred feet in the wild, and there are no dwarf varieties.

As Riccardo did with his home office in chapter 8, clearly delineate the spaces you use for specific purposes. Place a screen between the bedroom and living areas or a trunk at the foot of the bed. An entertainment center can also neatly separate these two locations.

A small apartment or condo usually has many square corners that can make the place look like it lacks depth. Tone down hard edges, recoup depth, and help chi to flow by placing a corner table, corner desk, or a treelike plant in a corner. A shadow box on a wall filled with miniature mementos will also provide depth as well as radiate your stellar personality. Shadow boxes, or what some now call "cabinets of curiosities," are enjoying a resurgence in popularity. The idea harkens back to Renaissance Europe, where the contents of these boxes gathered from one's travels were displayed for study, contemplation, and inspiration.

Other remedies include colorful rugs and throw pillows with undulating designs to create contrast and lend an individual touch. Finally, mirrors will help make your space look brighter and larger. Mirrors help deflect negativity and stagnating sha.

Dorms

Say you're a college student heading off to school for the first time. Undoubtedly, you'll share a tiny dorm room with a roommate or two whom you've probably never met. You won't have room to haul everything you want from home, so what should you bring to make dorm life easier?

As with a small apartment, storage room in a dorm is always problematic. But you're a smart college kid; you can meet this challenge! Go to the local lumber yard or hardware store and buy four cinder blocks to raise your bed so you can store bins full of stuff underneath. If your roommate agrees, make the beds into bunks to liberate more space.

While you're shopping for all those plastic under-the-bed and closet storage modules, don't forget a basket to tote your salon and bath products to and from the communal bathroom. A pair of flip-flops is practically mandatory for sliding in and out of the shower. While you're at the store, you might as well pick up both laundry and waste baskets.

Practical items you may want to tote from home or buy after you arrive include first aid and sewing kits, basic utensils, a bowl and a plate, paper towels, flashlight, double-sided removable sticky tape and hooks for hanging decorations on walls, a bottle opener, and basic cleaning supplies. A dry-erase board with markers and an eraser to hang on the door is another shrewd investment. Perhaps your roommate will spring for half of the expense.

If you have extra room, a couple of inexpensive small table lamps that radiate soft LED light will alleviate the harsh fluorescent overheads you may be stuck with. Consult with your roommate and see if you can divvy up that expense too. As with small apartments, a hollow ottoman is great for propping up your feet after a hard day at the library, and it doubles as a storage bin and coffee table. A capacious easy chair, available at a used furniture store, makes another snug addition. If it tips back, overnight guests, if allowed in the dorm, can also use it. If you still have space, consider a low side table. Keep it at your bedside to hold your cell and other devices, coffee mug, a book, tissue box, or whatever else you may need at your fingertips. It, too, can become a coffee table when needed. Check with the school well in advance of move-in day to find out what items they do and do not supply and allow. They will also provide useful information, such as if the room has a camper-size refrigerator or microwave.

Now for the fun part: making your humble abode your own. This is where you and your roommate can learn a lot about each other's backgrounds and tastes. The school can give you window and wall dimensions and a floor plan, which will help when you go to decorate. You and your roommate can discuss options, come to an agreement, and share expenses.

Think splashes of color and restful textures to mollify the white walls and angular spaces. As in small apartments and condos, a couple of plush throw rugs, perhaps with rippling designs, will go far toward warming what may be a cold linoleum-tiled floor. Perhaps you both want to invest in matching comforters, handsome throw pillows, or velvety drapery to mask Venetian blinds. You probably aren't allowed candles in your room due to the fire hazard, but LED lights that look like candles make a reasonable substitute.

It's courteous to consult with your roommate over wall decorations. Photos of loved ones, your place of origin, locations you've recently visited, etc., can help assuage pangs of homesickness and provide conversation topics for new friends and acquaintances. Posters also make a fun choice and are available at campus bookstores. A plant or two can invigorate the ambience and even substitute for the beloved pet who is probably not allowed. No matter what you do in the names of style and function, remember there's another person sharing this tiny space with you who also deserves a voice.

Hospital Rooms

The last twenty years or so have seen many renovations in hospital room decor because we now know that comfort and security play a key role in patients' recovery. Cheerfully painted birthing rooms and tastefully decorated cancer wards furnished with pretty curtains, old-fashioned rocking chairs, plush sofas, canopies of greenery, and state-of-the-art entertainment centers help make these spaces feel welcoming and harmonious.

In spite of these agreeable attentions to detail, the fact remains that the patient is in an unfamiliar environment away from the comfort and familiarity of home. People undergoing serious stress can be uplifted by personal touches that brighten their reduced space and mitigate some of the pain they are experiencing. More important, these niceties strengthen the patient's bond to others as well as to the outside world, keeping pangs of isolation at bay.

It's important to remember patients by sending or arriving with cards, flowers, or little gifts like CDs, DVDs, books, a plush robe, comfy slippers—whatever you know pleases them most. Once I brought a vial for aromatherapy oil on a necklace to a cancer patient friend. The oil was composed of eucalyptus and lavender to sterilize and freshen the air. She told me this was the best gift she received in the hospital because sniffing the fortifying aroma lifted her spirits.

Another friend who recently survived a bout of cancer told me she saved every card she received wishing her well for her operation and subsequent chemotherapy rounds and placed them along her hospital room window ledge. Once she got home, she displayed them all on her mantelpiece to cheer her during her recovery. She still keeps these mementos in a scrapbook.

I also believe in bringing something vibrant into the hospital room as an affirmation of life. I'm reminded of the famous short story by O. Henry, "The Last Leaf." In the story, it's late fall and a young artist dying of pneumonia stares out her hospital room window at an ivy plant clinging to the wall and slowly losing its leaves. She makes up her mind that when the last leaf falls, she, too, will die. An older artist friend decides to remedy the situation by secretly painting a lifelike green leaf on the wall that never falls. The pneumonia victim recovers. A plant may do more for a patient's psyche than we realize.

Fresh flowers are also welcome. Such an enchanting spray of color and effervescence they make! In a study performed at the University of Rochester, researchers concluded that flowers can make family members behave more agreeably toward each other and be more generous with their time. Maybe the same applies to hospital staff who enter the room.

Symbols of nature also help people feel more connected to others and to the world around them. This is especially important for dying patients who may feel they have been thrust into some kind of surreal environment. Alicia di Cristofano, a Reiki master who practices energetic touch for those who are sick and dying, agrees. She believes that even bringing in something as small as a leaf, shell, or pebble can help the dying stay connected to the world until they choose to exit. Alicia reminds us to keep necessary items like a cup, tissue box, clock, etc., within reach so the patient retains personal control over the immediate environment, no matter how reduced in size.

She also recommends that the visitor bring a personally significant item from the patient's home. Deposit it on a nearby small table along with similar items by way of erecting a kind of shrine. The visitor might perform a simple symbolic ritual by changing the items from time to time to help sustain interest in the shrine and remind the patient of home. Other things to consider bringing include framed photos, warm socks, or a favorite comforter or pillow. For myself, I like a fleecy bed jacket as I find there's always a draft in a hospital room.

Tiny Homes

Finally, I'd like to say a few words about the ultimate small spaces: tiny homes. They're popping up all over, from big cities to rural communities; on the seaside, mountainside, prairie, and wasteland; on the back of camper vans, and anywhere else you can conceive of. Why have these under-400-square-foot dwellings become so popular?

Several factors have combined to enhance the tiny home's appeal, principally the overcrowded housing market and limited personal finances. The urge to live a less-complicated life attracts many "back to the land" types. From former hippies to millennials, baby boomers, and environmentalists, these advocates believe small houses or residences on wheels give them the most freedom because of their simplicity. Plus these environmentally friendly dwellings can help reduce an individual's carbon footprint. Many tiny home builders and owners install a composting toilet, and wind or solar energy for heat and electricity.

Even some civic leaders and developers have nudged their way onto the tiny home bandwagon. For example, Denver, Colorado, is experiencing a homeless crisis, with currently five thousand people with nowhere to go. As part of the solution, the city built an experimental tiny home village. Inspired by other tiny communities around the country, Beloved Community Village, according to their website, is a "self-governing tiny home village whose purpose is to provide a home base and safe place" for the homeless. The village includes eleven tiny homes that will accommodate singles or couples. It also boasts communal areas for food preparation and gatherings, bathrooms, and showers. Alas, as of this writing, the tiny home community, which was in the experimental stage, has been moved and might eventually be demolished.

eleven

Connecting with Nature Indoors

In this chapter we'll forge a connection between your sanctuary and nature by evaluating indoor plants and woods suitable for your decor. Wood, like color, is an extensive topic, and I can only sand the surface here. In the resources section you'll find suggestions on where to go to broaden your knowledge of the subject. Here I'll also say a few words about plants to keep in your home and how to create an indoor kitchen herb garden so you can enjoy the taste and fragrance of a garden year-round.

You can bring a suggestion of the wild wood home even if you don't see yourself making a journey to faraway destinations. I know a woman who lives in an apartment with a sunny balcony. In the spring she puts so many houseplants there that it resembles a jungle. She hangs a sculpted sun on one wall and wooden flying geese on the other. With a hammock and a tabletop fountain nearby, she's created an ideal indoor-outdoor hideaway sheltered from the summer heat and neighbors' prying eyes, where both she and her kitty can snooze the afternoon away. If you have a balcony, have you ever thought of making it a comforting green space? How would you decorate it?

Plant a Kitchen Herb Garden

A wonderful way to invite the outdoors into your haven is to plant a kitchen herb garden. These miniature gardens require some maintenance, but it's well worth the trouble to have fresh, tasty herbs at your fingertips to season your food and to concoct herbal teas. All you need is a window where the sun shines for at least four hours a day all year. If you don't have this, think about installing a grow light.

Since each plant you choose will require slightly different soil and water amounts, the most convenient way to plant them is in separate pots. Each pot should have adequate drainage holes so the plants don't get waterlogged. Clay pots will give good drainage, but they dry out faster than the plastic ones. Cover the holes with a single layer of cheesecloth, teabag, or coffee filter so you don't lose the soil through the bottom. Saucers are mandatory to catch water overflow that can ruin your furniture, sill, or floor. If you set your plants close together, you can get away with putting a drainage pan under the pots instead of individual saucers.

Although most herbs tolerate average soils well, I recommend getting yours off to a good start by filling your containers with a mixture of organic potting soil and compost. You can choose to plant either seeds or already established plants.

I usually buy organic plants because seeds can be difficult to germinate. Rotate the pots every couple of weeks so they grow straight and strong and don't lean into the window, where they might freeze on a winter's night or get seared in the summer sun. Keep each herb well pruned so they don't grow into each other. This will be easy-peasy because you're always snipping off leaves to use for cooking or tea. Mist under the leaves to prevent them from curling in the dry air from heaters and air conditioners. Misting also discourages aphids, spider mites, whitefly, and other pests that hide out there. If your plants are in fairly small containers, you can give them a monthly treat by bathing them in the kitchen sink with the sprayer.

Six Tasty Kitchen Garden Herbs

Now to decide what to plant. This is always my biggest challenge because there are so many beautiful, useful, yummy herbs from which to choose. Here are six practically foolproof herbs for raising indoors. For more suggestions, see the botanicals section in the appendix.

Basil (*Ocimum basilicum*)

This annual grows approximately one to two feet tall. Basil requires well-drained soil and a lot of sun (six to eight hours daily), and the leaves need constant trimming to keep them from falling when the ambient temperature falls below 70 degrees. If you do this, you'll have fresh, spicy leaves to season your ethnic dishes. Basil flavors pasta, salads, soups, and a variety of tomato dishes.

This herb is known as a strengthener, anti-inflammatory, and antibacterial that treats warts, head colds, and loss of appetite. It also helps expel intestinal gas and reduces fluid retention. In folklore, basil is a protection plant. Hang a dried sprig over your doorway to discourage thieves and vandals from entering. Women once wore basil in their hair to attract a lover. Meditate on this plant for self-regeneration, achievement, mental activity, and love.

Chives (*Allium schoenoprasum*)

Chives are a perennial related to leeks, shallots, scallions, and garlic, only the taste is milder. This herb tolerates a wide variety of soils but, like basil, prefers full sun to really flourish. Chives grow on very thin stalks approximately one foot high and, if left to mature, blossom with light purple flowers. Snip off bits of this versatile botanical to flavor butter, cheese dishes, salads, soups, sour cream, stews, and vinegar. This herb is especially good for you because its organosulfur compounds help prevent colorectal, esophageal, stomach, and prostate cancers, and the choline helps with sleep and mood. The vitamin K content can increase bone density, and the plant's quercetin reduces cholesterol levels.

Like onions, chives are associated with the fire element and the planet Mars. Since they taste so mild, they are considered an herb that fosters tranquility. Meditate on this botanical to enhance your intuition and bring harmony into your environment.

Dill (*Anethum graveolens*)

A hardy annual that grows up to one foot tall without spreading, dill isn't fussy about soil. If you keep your plant indoors, know that it likes a sunny window. Both leaves and seeds are used in herbal medicine and cooking. The taste is like a combination of fennel, parsley, and caraway. In herbal medicine dill helps settle the stomach and expel intestinal gas. This common kitchen garden plant is known as the pickling herb because it's used to flavor breads, cakes, chicken, pickles, potatoes, sauerkraut, and seafood.

Dill is calming enough to promote a good night's sleep. Its essential oils fight inflammation and fungal infections. Medieval herbalists once recommended boiling the seeds in wine as an aphrodisiac and brain stimulant. In times gone by, brides tucked dill into their wedding bouquets to ensure a happy marriage. Meditate on dill to understand the true meaning of love and marriage and how to invite both into your life.

Lemon Balm (*Melissa officinalis*)

Also known as melissa, this easy-to-grow perennial enjoys both sun and partial shade and is not picky about its soil. Lemon balm is a spreader, so be sure to rein it in if you grow it outdoors. Indoors, it is the tallest of the recommended kitchen window garden herbs, soaring from two to four feet. This bushy plant also requires regular pruning. The leaf tastes deliciously refreshing, like lemon without the bite. Use the leaf in both herbal medicine and cooking.

In herbal medicine, lemon balm is an antiseptic, antioxidant, and gentle sleep inducer that also helps alleviate aching teeth, sore throat, and nausea. It's a good thing this botanical mitigates bee sting pain because its tiny white flowers are a bee magnet. Superstition dictates that if you drink a cup of lemon balm tea, you'll be able to predict the future. In some psychotherapy circles, this herb is used to stimulate past-life recall. For meditation, fragrant lemon balm is said to banish melancholy, rejuvenate the spirit, and improve communication skills.

Mint (*Mentha*)

Many species of this perennial mint grow throughout the temperate zones, including spearmint, apple mint, chocolate mint, orange mint, and pineapple mint. If I had to choose one all-around mint for my kitchen window garden, it would be peppermint (*M. piperita*). This plant grows up to 18 inches and spreads joyfully outdoors. If you keep the leaves trimmed indoors, it won't range out of control. Peppermint can tolerate a good deal of shade and poor soil but needs to be kept well-watered. The leaves are the part used both in medicine and cooking. The taste—no surprise—is minty, although some varieties have fruity overtones.

In herbal medicine, peppermint settles the stomach, is a decongestant, and relieves symptoms of cold, headache, toothache, sore throat, and arthritis. The refreshing scent and taste clear the mind and calm the nerves.

Peppermint tea is said to encourage prophetic dreams if drunk before bedtime. In cooking, peppermint extract is used to flavor lamb dishes as well as desserts, hard candy, and fudge. Peppermint adds an uplifting note to smoothies, juices, and other summertime drinks as well.

In myth, Pluto is said to have changed his wife's rival Mentha into a peppermint plant. Ancient Celts used to purify water with peppermint both for drinking and rituals. The dried herb makes a fine sachet to hang in your window shrine for good luck, happiness, parting of the ways, new beginnings, transformation, and release of anger. Meditate on peppermint when you wish to cement a business or personal relationship.

Parsley (*Petroselinum crispum*)

A biennial of the carrot family, parsley grows up to one foot tall and stays well-contained in its pot. This herb thrives in moist soil and partial sun, so it doesn't have to be in a south-facing window. The leaves and stems are used in cooking and herbal medicine and should be harvested before the flowers appear. The taste is fresh and slightly herbal. Add this versatile botanical to meat, chicken, vegetarian dishes, salads, and seafood. It is also a frequent garnish because of its beauty and digestive properties.

Besides aiding digestion, parsley is rich in vitamins A, B1, B2, B3, and C, and it is used to restore vitality and strength after an illness. Because of the association with strength, parsley leaves were often fashioned into victors' crowns at the Olympic Games in ancient times. Some people still believe that this botanical urges on racehorses. Parsley is also thought to facilitate meditation and divination. Meditate on parsley for better health and fortitude, and to achieve a cherished goal.

Other Indoor Plants

There are distinct advantages to adding plants besides the kitchen garden variety to your indoor decor. Here are some benefits living interiors provide:

- a plant of any kind will invigorate the chi in your sanctuary
- living interiors forge a connection between indoors and outdoors, bringing what you love best about nature home to you
- plants absorb carbon dioxide from the air and ease your breathing
- a large treelike plant can fill an empty corner, and smaller or hanging ones will enliven an otherwise dull shelf
- greenery increases the humidity in a room by releasing water into the air
- plants remove pollutants and freshen the air
- studies show that plants help focus the attention
- plants moderate hot air temperatures
- a living plant will visually brighten and beautify an interior by providing a focal point

Here are examples that will make you think you're living in a tropical paradise. A word of caution to pet owners and those with children: some houseplants are poisonous to animals and kids, so check for toxicity before purchasing any botanicals.

The Peace Lily (*Spathiphllum wallisi*)

This plant is happy in a well-lighted bathroom if it receives high humidity and is grown in moist, well-drained soil. Its elegant white flowers impart a peaceful energy, hence its name. As an added bonus, this beauty clears the air of the toxins acetone, alcohol, benzene, and formaldehyde. Meditate on the peace lily to calm down when someone or something has upset you and to gain general peace of mind.

English Ivy (*Hedera helix*)

This hanging vine with dark green leaves makes a lovely addition to any indoor environment. Place the pot on the corner of a shelf and watch the vine curl down to the floor. This bit of greenery does double duty in your home because it removes the most common airborne pollutants. In the office, if you work around formaldehyde, it will remove that toxin as well. This hardy vine can be planted outdoors and is a preferred plant for public spaces and for softening the look of exterior walls.

Other practical uses for this plant include boiling the leaves in water and applying externally for side aches and to the temples for headaches. A folk remedy for sunburn pain is to boil the leaves in butter, cool the mixture, and apply to the affected area.

English ivy has long been thought of as a resurrection plant because it grows in a spiral form. The entwined leaves composed the poets' crown and the wreath for the Roman god Bacchus. As a symbol of this deity's inspiration, ivy and silver fir ale were served during the Bacchanals. Because porous ivy wood was used to separate wine from water, tavern signs were often painted to show sprigs of ivy. Meditate on English ivy for inspiration, enhanced creativity, and deep friendships, especially bonds between women.

Food Plants

Besides emanating beauty and acting as a filtration system, some plants you can raise indoors provide nourishment beyond kitchen garden condiments. Mostly these consist of dwarf fruit trees like the date palm, fig, banana, orange, tangerine, kumquat, lemon, and lime. I keep a dwarf Meyer lemon in our piano room, where the flowers exude a bewitching fragrance that harmonizes with the music played there. The scores of lemons I harvest from the plant have a milder flavor than grocery store lemons—perfect for hot or iced tea and lemonade year-round—and citrus fruit is loaded with vitamins and minerals.

Full disclosure: no matter which citrus you choose, each is something of a prima donna, requiring more than the usual casual treatment for indoor plants. They all need 4–6 hours of sunlight daily and rich, well-drained soil that you must fertilize frequently. Regular watering without overwhelming the plant is also indicated. And you need to check both on top and under the leaves for insect infestations from aphids, mites, and the like.

Despite this, the enchanting aroma wafting from the blossoms and the delightful organic fruit you can harvest, not to mention the lush greenery, can make an investment in a dwarf fruit tree worth the trouble. If you're able to take it outdoors during the warmer months, this will help strength-en the tree. As meditation trees go, you can contemplate citrus for fertility, happiness, and purity. If you don't have room for one of these pretty ones in your haven, simply meditate on the fruit or a glassful of citrus juice.

A Blooming Desert: Cacti, Succulents, and Air Plants

I get it that many readers won't find the time or inclination to care for dwarf fruit trees. For you, may I suggest cacti and succulents? Being a desert plant, a cactus requires little water and nourishment only during their early spring blooming season. Cacti are slow growers that don't need repotting often; in fact, they thrive on neglect. However, this plant will need as sunny a spot as the fruit trees. There are dozens of varieties to choose from, some of which bloom yellow, pink, purple, or red in early spring. Meditation topics appropriate for your cactus include adaptability, courage, endurance, stoicism, and finding hidden treasure—perhaps you'll even discover a treasure in your mind!

Nobody will blame you if you decide you don't want to put up with cactus prickers. Instead, select a succulent, which also requires very little care. Agave, aloe, and yucca all spring to mind. One of my favorites is the jade plant (*Crassula ovata*). If allowed to grow, jade will become a tree, yet it is also appropriate as a bonsai. This plant is a popular housewarming gift in China because it's considered a lucky plant to have around. The thick ovate leaves look sculpted, and when in flower, the small blooms are a cheerful white or pink. Keep your plant in a sunny spot and water it every two weeks, and it will be content. Meditate on the jade to enhance your sanctuary's chi and improve your overall mental and emotional health.

Here are a few more handsome succulents that will brighten your space, whether it's big or small, and which double as conversation pieces. String-of-pearls (*Senecio rowleyanus*) is aptly named because strings of beads that resemble peas dangle down long stems in a way similar to English ivy. Pussy ears, also called the panda plant (*Kalanchoe tormentosa*), has a marvelous fuzzy texture. This sage-green plant with dark red edges grows just 12–18 inches tall. The zebra plant (*Haworthia fasciata*) is even shorter, at 5–6 inches. It's so named for the marked horizontal stripes on its swordlike leaves.

Another trending type of plant is the air plant (*Tillandsia*), which receives its name from the fact that it doesn't need soil to grow and receives most of its nutrients from the air. Therefore, some people mistakenly think that these plants require no care. Actually, when you first receive one, you must soak it for 30 minutes, then turn it upside down and let it dry completely overnight before putting it in its home. Then you need to monitor the weather carefully to know when to water, mist, or soak it, depending on the humidity and amount of light in the room. These pretty plants need good, bright light. If you go for a larger variety, it must be soaked rather than misted. No matter which variety you choose, you should allow it to dry completely before replacing it in its home position. Dry, brown curled up ends of leaves are a sign that you either watered too much or too little. And if you live in a dry climate, as I do, this is almost impossible to gauge. Frankly, even though these are lovely plants, I think you're better off with succulents; they're much less trouble.

Terraria

Are your living quarters so cramped that an array of plants won't fit? Maybe you're attracted to the idea of enjoying greenery around you but don't want to baby those fussy darlings along? A terrarium could provide the solution.

A terrarium is also called a glass garden or vivarium. It's a glass-sided receptacle, often with a glass top, that can be almost any size or shape—even a globe. Inside, plants are kept living in a controlled environment. As of this writing, terraria are trending big-time. Kits of all kinds are available at garden centers and hardware stores, and it's super easy to create your own.

Now for the fun part: you get to decide whether you want a cactus and succulent garden, a cool, moist garden, or a warm-temperature one. Just pick your plants. You might fill a cool, moist garden with anemones, aquamarines, ferns, lichens, and mosses. Plants for a warmer garden might include African violets, begonias, creeping figs, maidenhair fern, and peperomia. All the botanicals should have the same watering and light requirements. Also pay attention to color, leaf sizes and patterns, and different plant types. This is where your creativity with design can blossom.

To start your terrarium garden, line the bottom with a thin layer of sand or pebbles and spread charcoal evenly over this layer for drainage. Cover with a couple of inches of topsoil or potting soil. Space the greenery at approximately one-inch intervals—remember these are very short botanicals. Plant, and pat down with more soil. Once you're done, don't hesitate to move the plants around until you position them to please your aesthetic sense. Only water when the soil appears dry, and fertilize sparingly. Trim back leaves and branches so they don't hit the glass or dwarf each other. And that's all there is to it!

Bonsai

On the other extreme of plant tending, perhaps you're a minimalist or even a miniaturist who enjoys challenging your gardening skills and expressing your artistic flair with plants but you, too, are space-challenged. Think bonsai.

The bonsai originated in China over one thousand years ago. Under the influence of Zen Buddhism, the Japanese redeveloped the concept to what it is known as today: a realistic, miniaturized representation of nature in the form of a tree. A bonsai tree is not a dwarf. It's a normal-size tree; that is, a botanical with a woody trunk or thick stem made smaller by pruning, pinching buds, wiring branches, and restricting but not completely cutting off fertilizers. Although any tree may be shaped into a bonsai, those with smaller leaves are generally more successful because they're easier to prune. Bonsais range in size from 1 to 80 inches in height.

When shaping a bonsai, pay attention to what the front of the tree will look like because this is the angle from which it will be viewed. Bonsais are also meant to have a triangular shape because this mimics trees found in nature. The wider, more mature branches spread out toward the bottom, while the newer, smaller ones form a triangle, tapering to the top. Twelve basic bonsai styles and types exist, with many variations, including different themes such as seasons of the year or special landscapes. Keep in mind you're striving to achieve a graceful, balanced sense of nature unspoiled by human intervention.

Trees

Before delving into how both living trees and their wood can spruce up your indoor environment, I'd like to make a few general comments on these captivating large plants. In this way, you get a clear picture of what kinds of trees you might want to incorporate into your sanctuary and home.

Trees are large botanicals that form, or try to form, a central woody stem. They usually live for several years. Some trees, like the Lebanon cedar, have survived for two thousand years. Trees have a well-developed circulatory system through which they move sap. Measurable movements within this system include respiration, spasms, and electrical impulses. Incredibly, trees have been anesthetized with chloroform in order to transplant them with a minimum of shock. Indeed, trees are living, breathing entities.

At one time, most of Europe and North and South America were covered with dense forests out of which early tribes cut clearings to plant crops. Trees provide superior sources of food, shelter, weapons, and other necessities, and so our ancestors soon began to worship the tree spirits they imagined inhabited these towering timbers. After all, they reasoned, if trees were so fecund, they could also confer fertility on crops and humans.

Later, people consolidated their adoration from spirits of individual trees to forest deities who represented all trees. The Druids carried their reverence of trees so far as to abide in sacred groves. Remnants of this custom persisted into recent history. For example, from Colonial times onward, Christian ministers would deliver sermons from beneath oak and ash trees.

Our ancestors did well not to underestimate the importance of trees as some people do today. Because trees need carbon dioxide to synthesize food, they rinse the air of pollutants. As part of the synthesizing process, they release oxygen into the air we need to breathe.

Trees also absorb ground water, which, when released into the atmosphere, eventually falls as rain. A large eucalyptus tree will disgorge 82 gallons of water into the air over a twenty-four-hour period. On the other hand, a single almond from an almond tree requires 1.1 gallons of water to produce. Trees capture, protect, and fertilize topsoil, give shelter to birds that eat insect pests, and provide us with products for dyes, furniture, medicines, nourishment, paper, and weapons. As the highest form of vegetable consciousness, trees are considered guardians of our planet. Some people believe that large trees act as channels of universal forces of strength, stability, and continuity, and that they broadcast messages about the welfare of the planet.

A Personal Meditation Tree

One suggestion for incorporating nature into your sanctuary is to buy a small tree for meditation to uplift your spirits and guide you on your spiritual journey. A living tree inside your home, especially in your inner sanctum, will instill the space with a life force and grow with you as you mature in body, mind, and spirit.

Like most indoor plants, indoor trees are available to purchase year-round. Just be sure you buy one that's not expected to grow taller than your ceiling! To adopt a meditation tree, select one to fit your purpose. The following are particularly good choices: rosemary for remembrance, fig for immortality, dwarf citrus for cleansing, Norfolk Island pine for beginnings, dwarf banana for fertility, and palm for tranquility.

Although you can pot a seedling, it will take a long time to grow. So I suggest purchasing a reasonably priced, small, pre-potted tree available from most nurseries and gardening centers. Water and care for the tree according to the directions that come with it until you're ready to bless and dedicate it. A good time to perform this little rite is around Christmas, Hanukkah, Kwanzaa, Milad un Nabi, or the Winter Solstice, when the short days begin to grow longer in the Northern Hemisphere. Alternative auspicious dates are Earth Day or Arbor Day, which vary from year to year but are always in the spring.

On the day you've chosen, place the tree in its permanent location. Decide in advance on a name for your tree. You can call it anything you want. I recommend selecting a name that indicates a frequent meditation topic for you or a quality you wish to cultivate in yourself. For example, I've named more than one meditation tree Fortitude.

Write the tree's name in red ink on a small square of green paper and attach it with red thread to a branch. Declare aloud that by naming the tree, you have chosen it as your personal meditation tree. Promise to care for it always and ask that the blessings of the All-One be conferred upon it. As with any other plant, keep your tree watered, fertilized, free from insects, and trimmed of dead leaves and branches. At holidays, decorate your personal tree with colorful cloth strips to celebrate its beauty.

Two Superb Indoor Trees

Whether or not you choose them as meditation trees, here are two fine choices for bringing nature indoors. The Norfolk Island pine (*Araucaria heterophylla*) is not a pine, although its looks may fool you. This tree comes from an island off the coasts of New Zealand and Caledonia, so it's not cold hardy! To flourish, this jewel requires plenty of misting and bright, diffuse light. The tree is slow-growing but will still need repotting from time to time; outdoors, it can reach to one hundred feet. It makes an ideal meditation tree because it displays all the virtues of the *Pinus* genus without being related. (More on pines shortly.) Meditate on Norfolk Island pine to strengthen your resolve and ensure the success of new projects.

The rubber tree (*Ficus robusta, F. elastic*) is one of the most identifiable house and office plants, recognized by its broad, glossy, dark green leaves. This tree is native to subtropical Southeast Asia. Although it can tolerate a great deal of abuse, including fairly cold temperatures and dim light, as attested by my family's cavalier treatment of ours, this rambling tree glories in bright, diffuse light, a humid environment, moderate temperatures, regular fertilization, and a good monthly wipe-down of its leaves to remove dust. Your tree will thank you for your care by banishing most home and office toxins from the air, especially formaldehydes. Meditate on this gorgeous tree to attract good fortune and prosperity. Feng shui experts suggest keeping one in the southeast corner of your home or sanctuary, known as the wealth area.

The Power of Wood

If you feel you're cursed with a purple thumb when it comes to plants, do not despair! You can incorporate the power of trees into your sanctuary by including woods via paneling, flooring, textured wallpaper, furniture, or even a simple box or wooden statue. Wood vibrates with an energy that both uplifts and relaxes. It provides insulation, texture, and warmth, and highlights the beauty of the other decorative elements of your sanctuary. As to natural woods (excluding fiberboard, particle board, and plywood), there are two types: hardwoods and softwoods. In this section I'll describe two of each kind. Look for descriptions of other common woods in the appendix.

Hardwoods

Hardwoods come from slow-growing deciduous trees that produce seeds, lose their leaves in the fall, and leaf out again in spring. Because they grow slowly, their wood is dense and their color is usually dark. Such woods are prized for paneling, flooring, and furniture-making, and they tend to be more expensive than softwoods. Here are two striking hardwoods for you to consider.

Cherry (*Prunus* genus) is an outdoor fruit tree familiar to many. The wood is expensive but highly valued for making furniture, cabinetry, and sculpture. The grain is close, attractive, and requires no filler. The color varies from light brown to dark reddish-brown. It's challenging to work with this wood if you're thinking of carving a small statue from it. The fruit also provides an admirable cordial and syrup for coughs, colds, and sore throats, and is an alleged aphrodisiac. The inner bark relieves pain during childbirth and helps reduce postpartum hemorrhage. An infusion of the bark conditions hair, and the fruit is reputed to improve one's eyesight. When taken internally, the tasty berries help cause urine to flow.

One of my favorite ways to consume cherries is to pit a few and pop them into a smoothie. They also perk up breads, cakes, and ice cream. Meditate on cherries or the wood to improve your fortunes and your ability to adapt socially. Cherries in any form also cultivate compassion and spiritual awareness, and they help create the strength of will to meet any challenge.

Another magnificent hardwood is oak (*Quercus* genus). Acorns, the fruit of the oak, can be milled to make a bread rich in protein, which was a staple among the ancient Celtic and Germanic tribes. White oak wood, which actually is grayish-brown, is fairly expensive; red oak wood, with its reddish cast, is somewhat cheaper. Both types are hard and tough, which makes this wood the best for shipbuilding, furniture-making, and firewood. The handsome grain exhibits prominent rays or streaks. Oak bark is rich in tannins, which are ideal for treating hides and leather. A decoction of the bark alleviates vomiting and blood-spitting. Oak buds distilled in water quell fevers and dissolve kidney stones. The strongly antiseptic and astringent leaves are employed in remedies against hemorrhage, chronic dysentery, piles, and bleeding gums.

The oak is probably the most honored tree of ancient northern tribes because of its mighty girth and height, as well as its usefulness. It was sacred to all the thunder gods of myth, as well as to Zeus, Jupiter, and Llyr. It is said that King Arthur's round table was constructed from a single slice of a gigantic oak; a thirteenth-century reconstruction is still on display in England's Winchester Castle. Even today, Herne the Hunter is thought to haunt the oaks of Windsor Forest, and stories of other haunted oaks survive throughout Britain.

The superstitious of times gone by believed that this tree drew lightning and that fairies could enter a house built of oak through the knotholes. The French used to build chapels from oak, and holy oaks still exist in West Saxony and

Westphalia. The nuns of St. Brigit of Kildare maintain a "perpetual shrine of the oak" with an ever-burning fire, a tradition rooted in the times of worship of the fire goddess. Oak is symbolic of a door swinging on its hinges, welcoming in the first half of the year, hence its association with Janus, the two-faced god of beginnings, doorways, and endings. Meditate on this robust, resilient tree to divine which doors are opening for you. The enduring oak tree teaches by example how to be sturdy in body, mind, and spirit.

Softwoods

The second category of wood for your sanctuary is softwoods. They are lighter in color than hardwoods and, as their name indicates, are less dense and therefore are more susceptible to nicks and scrapes. Nevertheless, some of these woods are widely used for paneling, flooring, and furniture. Their light color helps give a room a contemporary look. They are generally less expensive than hardwoods. Here are two examples.

Aromatic cedar (*Cedrus* genus, *Thuja* genus) freshens closets and banishes moths with its clean, woodsy aroma. This moderately expensive, light red–colored wood also makes coffins and storage chests, totem poles, and dugout canoes, but it is too soft to be suitable for furniture. If you use cedar to panel a closet, keep it unpainted. If you're making a storage chest, coat the outside with a clear stain to accentuate the handsome grain and protect it from dings. In ancient times cedar incense was used as a fumigant. Meditate on cedar to appreciate the gifts you already possess and to be prosperous and long-lived.

White pine (*Pinus* genus) is a versatile tree with a high commercial value as timber. Both Colonial and modern furniture, as well as unfinished furniture, are manufactured from it. The wood is moderately priced and looks handsome with its cream to yellowish-brown color and close grain with clearly marked growth rings. You can stain it to match existing furniture in your home. The resin is an ingredient of turpentine and some incenses and composes violin rosin.

If you've never eaten pine nuts, you're in for a gourmet experience. Pine nuts are a staple of many Southwest Native American tribes and are ingredients of several tasty dishes. Veterinarians prepare medications from its bark and needles that are antiseptic, stimulant, and diuretic. When inhaled, crushed pine needles stimulate the mucous membranes and respiratory system. Because the needles contain phenols, aromatherapists use the extract to reduce stress. Pine oil is an ingredient of liniments and plasters and makes an invigorating bath.

Pine was one of the Irish chieftain trees of yore. It is also considered a goddess tree and is associated with birth and rebirth. In Japan this tree symbolizes the New Year. Many cultures have considered the pine a timeless tree that reminds humans of our very small place in the universe. The needles are an ingredient of shamanic incenses because some Native American tribes see the pine as a peace symbol. The Iroquois burn the cones and needles to banish nightmares and ghosts. Meditate on pine to be protected from illness, open the third eye to enlightenment, and gain tranquility.

twelve

Secret Gardens

We've been spending a lot of time inside, so I think we're ready to escape the house for a breath or two of fresh air. Grab your windbreaker, gloves, and mud boots, and let's go! In this chapter you'll learn how to construct a sanctuary in your garden or on your patio. If you live in an apartment or other situation that prohibits having an outdoor garden, or are allergic to plants, skip to the next chapter.

Your Dream Garden

I once thought it would be a terrific idea to have a garden that bloomed all white. So on the strip of land next to my house, I planted masses of white-flowering tulips, crocuses, sweet-smelling hyacinths, and daffodils, along with white astilbe, vibernum, miniature white rose bushes, and fragrant nicotiana. The crowning glory of my masterpiece, planted in the center, was a fragrant dwarf magnolia. I loved that garden but wouldn't repeat the design today. My tastes have changed, and a one-color garden no longer appeals. Most personal sanctuaries are supposed to be works in progress anyway, and they change as you do.

As you read this chapter, I'd like you to contemplate your dream garden. Would it bloom all white or do you prefer blue, red, yellow, orange, or purple? Would you rather mix colors? Is your ideal garden filled with annuals that attract bees and butterflies? Do you want a garden that requires little care, with lots of perennials to shelter wildlife? Maybe you dream of a fragrant garden or a plot that showcases one kind of plant, such as roses. Then again, perhaps you're interested in growing culinary and healing herbs, which—not coincidentally—is the next topic on our agenda.

Create an Herb Garden Retreat

If your home has room for a garden, however small, and you are blessed with at least one pale-green thumb, take a tip from Celtic and Saxon herbalists and medieval monks of centuries gone by and devote some space to an herbal retreat.

Typical contemporary home gardens consist mainly of the usual suspects: tomatoes, cucumbers, radishes, spinach, and squash, with a few annual herbs tucked here and there in pots. This was not always the case. Gardens of long ago were bursting with native herbs. Vegetables were almost unknown, at least in northern climes, and herbs were prized because they were useful and provided culinary and scented delights. From herbs, people made seasonings for meats and concocted tisanes, syrups, elixirs, ointments, medicines, distilled waters, and washing balls. Pomanders and scented bags fragranced their linens and homes. Salads were comprised entirely of herbs, without any lettuce.

At first, these early gardens consisted mostly of conglomerations of seeds planted and left to germinate, grow, and spread without vigorously reining them in. Despite the later Victorians' mania to tame nature in the garden, a small area was always put aside for herbs to grow almost at random. Only in contemporary times, when many have lost interest in physic gardens, has this garden feature been largely eliminated.

Although evolving gardens eventually relegated herbs to afterthoughts in leftover corners, some constants remained. Growing herbs for scent, tea, medicine, and, most importantly, to provide a tranquil space for rest and meditation still prevails in some places, mainly in organic gardens. During the heyday of herbal gardening, botanicals were arranged in rectangular enclosures surrounded by walls or thick hedges. Medieval monks were especially fond of cutting recesses in the hedges or walls to make seats from the thick turf that also flourished at the borders. Another change was the addition of sundials and fountains to attract birds and beneficial insects. Eventually, eye-catching flowers that provided church decorations became garden staples, and flowers and herbs were separated into different plots.

The monks liked to plant a small tree like an elder, willow, or rosemary bush to provide a focal point as well as protection from the elements. As time passed, herb seeds were sewn in raised beds, often with one type of plant per bed to keep them from crowding each other. The Victorians and others trained herbs to grow in decorative knots, mazes, and spirals. A kind of arbor called an herber might be erected as well. An herber consisted of simple poles over which sweetbriar, dog rose, or wisteria might be trailed with a seat beneath for the visitor to pause and enjoy the fragrance.

If you travel to New York City, you'll find something similar at the Metropolitan Museum of Art's Cloisters, located in Fort Tryon Park. The outdoor area has four herb gardens laid out in the medieval fashion with hundreds of plants that were available during the Middle Ages. Against one wall is a magnificent espaliered pear tree—that is, a tree that has been trained to grow on a trellis. If your yard is small, you might consider this a space-saving way to plant at least one bush or dwarf tree.

I'm not suggesting you install an entire herbal landscape, but you may want to consider planting a few of these botanicals in a sunny spot. You'll attract butterflies, bees, birds, ladybugs, lacewings, praying mantis, and other beneficial insects that will make short work of garden pests. Watching these tiny creatures go about their business is a real treat. Moreover, in planting and tending a garden, you'll get healthy exercise outdoors in the sunshine and fresh air. Who knows? You may even end up harvesting some fresh seasonings, tea ingredients, and medicinal botanicals. You'll know where they came from and that they're free of pesticides. More to the point, you'll have crafted a perfect little retreat for yourself.

For me, a six-foot-by-six-foot plot works well, but your herb garden can be any size. Dig the area to a depth of at least one foot. Smooth out dirt clods with a hoe and rake, and add a few organic amendments such as compost, well-rotted manure, and leaf mold. Work the amendments well into the soil so it becomes easy to plant and even easier for the botanicals to take root. Luckily, most herbs can thrive in fairly poor soil, but it still makes sense to give your darlings a good start in life. As time goes by and you want to fertilize, use an organic product so you don't kill off beneficial bugs and birds. Chemical fertilizers produce plants that, while showy, have watery, thin cell walls that wildlife doesn't find very palatable. Besides, you may actually want to harvest some of these plants to consume, and it goes without saying you should never use pesticides on herbs. Beneficial bugs will handily destroy most pests. A birdhouse and/or feeder and seating as simple as a lawn chair make superb additions. Now you're ready to plant.

My idea of planting herbs is somewhat slapdash in the sense that I don't do raised beds and gravel walkways, nor am I particular about preventing one herb from growing into another. I pay attention to height, placing taller herbs behind shorter ones so the smaller plants don't get too much shade. For the same reason, I also put taller plants on the north side. To learn which plants grow best in your area, go to the Lady Bird Johnson Wildflower Center online at wildflower .org and search their native plant database. I live in Colorado, one of the most challenging states in which to garden, given the altitude, poor soil, dry climate, gale-force winds, and huge temperature variations throughout the year. So if you follow some of my planting suggestions, you may end up doing okay.

If there's room, you might want to locate a small tree or bush in the center such as a rosemary or elder. Against the north wall you can plant red and black raspberries, two of my and the birds' favorites. In front of the bushes, think of locating lavender, sage, angelica, milkweed, and maybe some lemon balm. Moving toward the front, consider planting the somewhat shorter chamomile, borage, fennel, coneflower (echinacea), yarrow, and monarda. In a front row, you might grow mint (this plant is good to place under taller plants, as it likes some shade), strawberries, chives, red clover, different lettuce varieties, and thyme.

As a front border, a sun-loving annual like pot marigold looks cheerful and acts as a barrier against bugs. If you prefer, set a row of spicy-scented pink, red, and white carnations (once known by the charming name "gillyflowers"). Both these kinds of flowers are edible. To round things out, pop in a couple of potted kitchen herbs like dill, parsley, and basil. If an errant sunflower seed or two manages to find its way into the plot, baby it along. Water everything well and keep the plants weed-free. Now sit back and watch them sprout, flourish, and enjoy each other's company. To learn about more herbs, see the appendix under the botanicals heading.

To enhance your experience in your herbal retreat, you might buy an identification book on birds, butterflies, and insects, or keep a journal to log changes in weather and what kinds of wildlife visit your sanctuary and when. If you're artistic, you may even get involved in sketching some of this delicately beautiful greenery.

Fairy Henges: Perfect Hideaways for the Kids

One day, my friend Sara was gazing out her kitchen window at the boring, grassy backyard and the idea struck her that she could construct a fairy henge there for her three children. That way, she could keep an eye on them while they played, teach them about the healing power of herbs, and at the same time have a family retreat.

A fairy henge is a small, circular garden, usually built in the wild, that is alleged to attract fairies. Since Sara's children were fascinated by fairy tales and myths, the henge would be an exciting place where they could let their imaginations run wild—and she wouldn't have to drive them elsewhere for recreation.

So Sara went about laying out a nine-foot-diameter stone patio bounded by a moss-covered wall, low enough to use as seating. She allowed for some crannies in the walls to hide away secret treasures or make offerings to the fairies.

Fairy henges often are constructed to include at each compass point representations of the four elements of nature— air, fire, water, and earth. Sara planted a big mugwort bush in the east to block part of the view to the backyard and help the children imagine they were playing in the wild. She positioned trees at the other cardinal points—a fir in the south, an apple in the west, and a mountain ash in the north. Potted plants, herbs, and bulbs distributed randomly around the space enhanced the wilderness effect and added more privacy.

Naturally, the children have had their say about what goes into the garden. Right now, Sara is helping them build a fairy house, a mini sanctuary very much in progress. They're filling it with tiny so-called fairy plants of lore such as lily of the valley, chamomile, fairy bells, nasturtium, miniature thyme, and a cherry tomato.

On summer evenings, the family gathers around the circle to toast marshmallows at the outdoor fireplace Sara's husband built. Mom lights candles and spins tales and everyone shares their hopes and dreams. In short, this space fulfills many functions. It's an untamed but safe haven in an urban setting where Sara's children can play and that doubles as a quiet late-night haven for the parents. It's a horticultural classroom and retreat where the family can bond and create memories.

Do you have a little one who adores fairies and would like to participate in such a project? Even if you don't, you're never too old yourself to be enchanted by fairies, pixies, brownies, and elves by creating your own fairy henge.

Treehouses

If your yard has the right kinds of trees and you're dexterous with a hammer and saw, why not build a treehouse? Treetop playhouses have certainly evolved from when I was a child. I remember my father picking through the junkyards for lumber scraps and using discarded carpet to cobble together what I thought was a pretty neat retreat—and still do. Nevertheless, changes are blowing in the wind for the treehouse business.

Today you can buy kits or prefabricated treehouses or have one professionally designed and installed according to your budget. You can even select a theme for your leafy getaway, such as a pirate ship, old woman in a shoe, or medieval castle. The treehouse concept has expanded further to embrace adults. This little space hidden away in the branches can become a haven to relax, entertain, and perhaps use as an auxiliary office. Some handy homeowners install plumbing and electricity and convert the treetop eyrie into a guest bedroom—a far cry from the rickety ladder of my childhood that led to the mostly open-air shack where you needed to repeat the secret code words before you were allowed admittance!

If you're determined to build your own, here are a few tips. Do most of the construction on the ground instead of in a swaying tree. You won't need to clamber up and down a precarious ladder for a forgotten tool, and your sawhorses will be right there where you need them. When working in the tree, always store your tools in a tool belt—that's what it's for—and loop an extension cord around a limb. Investigate thoroughly the kinds of trees capable of holding a treehouse and look for the lightest possible wood to use for building the structure. Some treehouse experts suggest using a lightweight aluminum shell.

Begin with a sturdy platform that allows for movement from the branches so you don't harm the tree. To further minimize damage, the structure that sits on top should not be attached to the trunk. Some lovely treehouses have been erected on the trunks of already dead trees. Finally, consult a certified arborist to guide you on how to limit tree damage. After all, you are doing this, in part, to honor trees, not destroy them.

If you prefer to visit or stay in someone else's unique hideaway, plenty of treehouse B&Bs and hotels doing brisk business worldwide will accommodate you. For instance, you could overnight at the Cedar Creek Treehouse in Ashford, Washington. This place is not for those leery of heights. Standing fifty feet off the ground in a magnificent western red cedar tree, this B&B is equipped with a large bedroom, observation room, and kitchen.

For the even more adventurous, try the Treetops Hotel in Aberdare National Park, Kenya, where you can sleep overnight while on safari. From the lounge, you get a bird's-eye view of elephants, lions, and other jungle creatures visiting their watering holes.

In central Tokyo, go for tea at Taka's Treehouse Cafe and Bar. Visitors extol its virtues as an oasis of greenery encased in an asphalt jungle. For more places to visit and directions on how to build an environmentally friendly treehouse, I recommend the fully illustrated book by Pete Nelson entitled *New Treehouses of the World* (Abrams Publishing, 2009).

Living Walls and Roofs

A unique way to enhance your outdoor space is to plant a living wall. Also known as a green facade, it is a carpet of plants grown in modules and anchored against a vertical structure like a wall, fence, or trellis. The plants are rooted in the ground at the base, and if the structure is tall, also in elevated planters set at intermediate levels. Extensive vertical gardens with their own complex recycling water systems are trending in big cities where high-rise buildings abound. You can visit striking examples of both interior and exterior living walls in public spaces from Singapore to New York, Paris, Sao Paulo, and Turin. One example that's easy to spot because it's located directly across from the Buckingham Palace Mews in London is the exterior side wall of the Rubens at the Palace Hotel. The greenery climbs up the brick, covering the facade.

Living walls are no longer confined to clinging ivy as in the past. Today a remarkable variety of vegetation grows on these panels, ranging from perennial ground covers and flowers to herbs, small shrubs, and edible plants like strawberries and tomatoes. The benefits of planting living walls and their cousins the roof gardens are enormous. Besides their aesthetic value, these green spaces create photosynthesis and reduce the heat emanating from tall buildings and concrete with their ability to naturally cool the air through evapotranspiration. Plants also trap the particulates and gases generated by vehicular traffic and industry and help diminish urban noise pollution. Moreover, these gardens create a biodiversity that attracts beneficial insects and birds and helps produce a healthy environment for city dwellers.

Many building owners realize the multiple benefits of living walls and roof gardens, especially since these remedies improve energy efficiency by lessening temperature fluctuations. The structures seal off the incoming air around doors, windows, and cladding by decreasing the deleterious effect of wind pressure. Although money is spent to design, erect, and maintain green walls and roofs, this expense is offset in part, by the boost to the local economy that creates jobs for those who design, build, and maintain the gardens. The advantages of green structures are considered so valuable that Denver, Colorado, has put into effect the Green Roof Initiative. Resoundingly approved by voters, the initiative requires all buildings over 25,000 square feet to install rooftop gardens that cover at least 20 percent of the roof with greenery. This law applies to both new and existing buildings, with exceptions made for some historic structures and schools that can't afford the cost.

There's no need to embark on such a grandiose project for your backyard. But you can adapt these big structures to any size outdoor space, even an apartment balcony if it gets enough light. Just think small. Start with a simple trellis and stick the legs into large pots filled with soil. Plant from the ground up, and attach more pots farther up the trellis if you want. Or keep it simple and install a pre-planted module that already contains the seeds and soil or that may be fully grown. It can take several seasons for a vertical wall to mature, so you may not want to wait for the plants to become fully grown from seed. Several garden companies provide fully grown modules. You can even choose the kind of greenery you want—groundcover, ferns, vegetables, flowers, and the like.

Thousands of vertical and rooftop green spaces are cropping up all over the world. Here are a few of my favorite rooftop destinations to visit for inspiration:

The roof garden at the Rockefeller Center in New York City is magnificent but only open sporadically throughout the year. If you find it closed, visit the roof of the nearby Metropolitan Museum of Art. Sip the tea they serve while gazing out over Central Park.

The Waldspirale Garden in Darmstadt, Germany, is aptly named. It's located on a ramp shaped like a spiral that winds around the outside of a twelve-story fairytale-like apartment complex. At the top of the ramp, a café awaits visitors to refresh themselves and view the masses of shrubs, grasses, and flowers.

The Kaiser Center Roof Garden in Oakland, California, sports an enormous green roof space that includes lawns, a small lake with a little wooden bridge, a fountain, and tree-lined borders.

In London, I recommend the Barbican Conservatory located at the Barbican Center, a thriving area that includes a concert hall, theaters, and galleries along with private apartments. The roof has an enclosed garden on two levels housing more than two thousand varieties of tropical plants. You'll think you've been transported to the Amazon!

Iberian Patio Gardens

On Europe's Iberian Peninsula, where Spain and Portugal are located, patio gardens flourish. Their design reflects the melding of two early conquering cultures, the Romans and the Moors. Both of these civilizations ruled over Iberia for centuries. The Romans came first (205 BCE–500 CE), followed by the Moors, who reigned from 711–1492 CE.

The Romans introduced homes built in a square around an interior patio, called an atrium, with a central fountain or well. They covered the patios with tiles, stones, and bricks. This design provided a way to enjoy the outdoors in seclusion and safety. The Moors expanded on this design by arranging the tiles in elegant geometrical patterns, which they extended to fountain decorations. They also refined the concept of a patio garden as a sacred space for relaxation, contemplation, and renewal. They added greenery and scent with orange and lemon trees, roses, jasmine, and potted and hanging planters cascading with flowers. Irrigation canals running between the garden and the interior furnished a primitive but successful kind of air conditioning. The Moors called their havens "heaven on earth."

Today's Iberian patio gardens, many of which you can visit, present a feast for the senses as well as a blissful retreat. Let Iberian gardens inspire you to perhaps incorporate some of these same features into your sanctuary design, such as gleaming tiles, a burbling bird bath, or aromatic flowers. You might even install a "canal" in the form of a humble soaker hose.

Some Alternatives:
Journey into Nature

If messing around with soil, pots, and fertilizer isn't your cup of tea, yet you enjoy the aromas and beauty of plants, why not go for a walk? Journey out into nature, even if it's to the park down the road. Many of our cities have dedicated open spaces to be used as refuges from the noise, traffic, concrete, and congestion of city life. If you still your mind and pay attention, you'll be surprised how, even with people and vehicles milling about, the grasses and flowers, bushes, and especially the trees will speak to you. Following are two illustrations of places that may help ease your life back into sync with the natural rhythms and cycles of the planet so you can find the harmonious balance you're striving for in your home sanctuary.

The Lan Su Chinese Garden

The Lan Su Chinese Garden takes up a mere city block in the heart of Portland, Oregon. Once you enter, if it weren't for the occasional city noises that manage to penetrate the tranquility, you may feel you've time traveled back to the sixteenth-century home and garden of a wealthy Chinese merchant.

This garden was built in 2000 CE with materials, including 500 tons of rock, mostly imported from China. Three hundred different plant species and cultivars have been planted there. As you meander around the premises, you come upon various authentically reproduced rooms and courtyards. They include a scholar's study, lounge house, teahouse, terrace, pavilions, a waterfall on a rock mountain, and more.

There is also a miniature lake set in the middle of the garden. The guidebook states: "The ebb and flow of seasons, the changing weather—even the shifting patterns of light throughout the day—can dramatically alter the garden's appearance." You get a fantastic view of this lake from the teahouse. Sit at one of the open-air windows and survey the garden and the reflections on the lake from the city's buildings beyond the confines of the garden walls while sipping the excellent tea. I think the Lan Su represents an ideal outdoor sanctuary everybody can enjoy.

Native American Sweat Lodges

To many Native Americans, the sweat lodge is the ultimate sanctuary—a place of spiritual refuge to pray, meditate, gain wisdom, and purify body, mind, heart, and spirit. Like many other havens described in this book, the sweat lodge is where a person can contact spiritual entities, share thoughts with others, grow, experience release from pain, and heal, all in safety. Native Americans can be fairly generous as to whom they invite to share their lodge. If you go, make sure you have their permission. I don't advocate trying to build your own. As you will soon see, it is an arduous process to construct one, and attendance at a ceremony can be dangerous because of heat, steam, and fire unless you are guided by a pro.

You may have run across a sweat lodge, especially if you've traveled off the beaten path throughout the Southwest. The small structure stands only four to five feet high and looks like a dome. It is constructed by bending flexible saplings from trees like aspen and willow and strapping them together with rawhide strips, grass, roots, or mud as a cover to form a shell that is typically, although not always, ten feet in diameter. Then it is covered with anything handy—blankets, plastic sheeting, tarps, carpet—to help retain the heat. By tradition, the entrance is in the east, the direction of sunrise and beginnings. A fire pit approximately two feet in diameter and one foot deep is dug inside in the center of the lodge. Another fire pit is located outside to heat the stones brought in during the ritual. To generate steam, water is made available to pour over the hot stones once they are moved to the interior pit.

Then the floor is swept of dirt and debris and covered with cedar boughs, sage, or other fragrant leaves for the comfort and cleanliness of the participants. This amenity is kept safely away from fire pit. Finally, an altar is erected between the entrance and fire pit. A pole with a skull on top is there to alert participants not to fall into the pit and remind them that only the official fire keepers are permitted to pass by. At the base of the pole, a small altar displays items sacred to the clan, as well as feathers, herbs, shells, and other decorations.

Before attending a ceremony, participants are urged to fast for twenty-four hours. Before entering, they are smudged with herbs. Once inside, they may bring an offering of tobacco to place on the fire and render a prayer to honor the Great Spirit. They may be offered a puff on the *chanumpa*, also known as a peace pipe. After these preliminaries, participants crawl around the lodge in a clockwise direction until they find a place where they will sit cross-legged against a wall during the ceremony.

Often four rounds of ceremony are experienced, each accompanied by freshly heated stones and steam. Anybody who feels unable to bear the heat and steam is allowed to leave at any time. Round one recognizes the spirit world, while round two recognizes positive qualities such as courage and honesty. Round three shows an appreciation of prayer and knowledge, and round four salutes growth and healing. Between rounds participants go outside to cool off, preferably in a cold stream, if one is nearby. During the rounds, participants share their thoughts, feelings, hopes, and fears, and petition Father Sky, Mother Earth, and various spirits to provide solutions to their problems. On leaving the lodge after completion of the ceremony, some participants claim the experience feels like returning to a womb—dark, warm, moist, soft, and safe. The ultimate sanctuary indeed!

Don't worry if Portland or Iberia or a sweat lodge aren't in your travel plans. Instead, check around for a local butterfly house, a college campus where botanical research is ongoing, or even a nearby greenhouse. Butterfly houses are open to the public, and if you talk to those in charge of the other venues, you may find they conduct tours of their facilities. And don't forget that college campuses often have large, landscaped, easily accessible areas.

thirteen

Home Sweet Home Away from Home

Now that we've moved out of the house, in this chapter we'll determine how to establish a sanctuary in an unfamiliar setting and brainstorm ideas on how to make your office—whether at home or away—a productive, cheerful, comfortable space in which to work. I also interview a small business owner who shares tips on how to make her store a sanctuary for all. Later, I offer a few words on how to ease the transition to an international relocation and discuss how to manage a move when you're on a budget.

I'd like you to close your eyes and call to mind how it feels to travel in another city, even another country. You've spent all day at a conference attending talks, making a presentation, developing important contacts, catching up with colleagues, and perhaps also improving your mind. Time to hurry home and tumble into your warm, cozy bed.

Wait—you can't! You open your hotel room door to a stark vanilla-white interior, made even more white by the fact that the thermostat is set at a chilly fifty degrees and the windows are hermetically sealed. The bed is a lumpy mattress, and the sterile bathroom overwhelms you with its antiseptic odor and fluorescent lighting. You can't even manage to wrestle your clothes onto the theftproof hangers. Frustrated, you flop down on the lump, sigh, and prepare to spend an uncomfortable night staring at the tube or rolling around fitfully in bed trying to sleep. Guess what? It doesn't have to be that way.

Debug Your Hotel Room

Here's a primer on literal debugging. It's an unpleasant feature of contemporary societies worldwide that bed bugs are on the increase; in fact, their population has exploded. Bed bugs seem to be everywhere, not only in disreputable dives but in the best hotels and public spaces such as libraries and waiting rooms. While I can't do much to help you out in public venues, I can suggest various remedies for your hotel bed.

A bevy of products to combat bed bugs has proliferated. Some are safe for you to be around; others, not so much. A few will cost you a lot. Yet one of the safest, cheapest, and most effective remedies out there is something completely natural that you can prepare for yourself for less than one dollar. I'm talking about lavender water. Before I leave on a trip, I fill a three-ounce plastic travel spray bottle with a half ounce of lavender essential oil and top it off with water. You can substitute eucalyptus oil, which is somewhat cheaper, or combine a quarter ounce of both oils.

When I enter the room, after carefully placing my suitcase on a stand, I go to the bed and remove the coverlet and decorative pillows, which I place neatly on a chair I'm not going to use. I open my bag, take out the lavender water, and shake the bottle vigorously to evenly distribute the oil. I quickly take off the blanket and top sheet and methodically spray the sheets, pillows, and blankets. Since lavender and eucalyptus are essential oils, they evaporate fairly quickly without staining fabrics or surfaces. More important, they banish bed bugs. And they leave a lovely, clean fragrance lingering in the room for a short time that smells like freshly washed sheets.

There's more you can do to debug the room—at least metaphorically—and make it feel like home. Rather than sticking to the barebones essentials, pack one or two indulgent items like a packet of bubble bath, a favorite shampoo or aftershave, French milled soap, a miniature bottle of perfume, or that new facial mask you've been wanting to try; whatever strikes your fancy. A friend of mine who travels nonstop always remembers to bring his favorite coffee mug. Set the indulgences on the bathroom vanity shelf to personalize your space.

Pack some spiritual assistance essentials in your traveling altar, too. (You *have* created a traveling altar from chapter 4, haven't you?) Options can include a small plug-in aroma diffuser or an aroma inhaler. For inhalers, you can buy a mixture of essential oils at aromatherapy emporiums or drugstores or make one of your own by buying a blank (empty) inhaler with a pad on which to place a couple drops of oil.

Essential oils are a must. Unlike synthetics, they don't stain, and most have high evaporation rates. (Patchouli is a notable exception.) This detail is important because when you check out, you don't want to leave any aromas lingering behind for future guests. Some scents that help relax are chamomile, eucalyptus, lavender, rose, and vanilla.

You can also try aromas that remind you of home. For example, do you live near water? Then a fragrance like bay leaf, which is associated with the ocean or a lake, might be appropriate. Since I live in the forested mountains, I make a blend of fir and sage, although I could also easily select copal and pine. If you use a diffuser, don't worry that you'll set off the smoke alarm because diffusers don't produce smoke. If you bring along scented votive candles and their glass containers, make sure you don't light them near a smoke detector, not that they are likely to cause it to go off, but it's worth being cautious. Also, if you do light a votive, be vigilant about putting it out after you have meditated, and never leave it burning in the room when you're away. Hoteliers frown on guests who set the room on fire!

Another item to drop into your bag is a tiny totem, statue, or other comforting symbol. A snapshot of a loved one or pet can also fit snugly into your traveling altar. Make it a physical photo in a frame—not something you've shot with your phone and have to scroll through to find it—and set it on the bedside table. A physical photo seems more permanent; it's always there to greet you when you enter the room. Bring something organic from home, too, like pebbles from your garden, a shell from the nearby ocean, or a vial of soil. Round out your traveling kit with a little book of devotional readings or meditations, a portable CD player, or a soothing recording of nature sounds, jazz, classical, or rock—whatever relaxes you.

Here's a little routine to clear the air. Plug in the aroma diffuser. If you've brought a votive, light it and stand in the center of the room. Lift the votive in both hands and cast the light around all four corners of the room. Visualize that you are purifying the air and filling it with light. If you feel the need, recite aloud a prayer, mantra, or any comforting quotation from your spiritual background. Take a few moments to picture the room as a safe and restful haven that will allow you to relax and recharge your batteries after a taxing business meeting or busy day of sightseeing. Repeat this procedure in the bathroom, but leave the aroma diffuser diffusing away in the bedroom. When you leave the bathroom, extinguish the votive.

For in-room refreshment, I take a colorful square of material as a kind of tablecloth from my kit and spread it on a table or dresser to foster harmony and give the place a homey touch. Then I bring out my tea things, including a proper china cup, my own metal spoon, a selection of teas kept fresh inside a metal pencil box, and my own electric pot. Many hotel rooms supply brewing pots, but most of them smell of coffee. This may be fine if you're brewing coffee, but it doesn't go down well with tea drinkers. In my opinion, no brewing pot does as good a job as my own, anyway, and I prefer my own fresh teas. You may want to do the same thing with coffee.

While I'm waiting for the water to boil, I slip into comfortable sweats, cotton socks, and house slippers, and take a favorite book from my suitcase or bring it up on my device. Then I sit and unwind with a cuppa and have a good half hour's read. Pretty soon I'm feeling so snug and secure, I might be in my own bedroom—well, almost.

Despite taking these measures, you may still feel uncomfortable in a different environment, whether it's a hotel room or a friend's or relative's spare bedroom. My recommendation in these cases is to do a little protection ceremony before retiring. Recite the Lord's Prayer, meditate, or do some other series of actions that reflect your spiritual beliefs. When I find myself in new surroundings, I carry out a procedure from my own spiritual path, which includes reciting, either aloud or silently, the names of the archangels. This process takes around ten minutes to complete. Here's an extreme example of how performing a protection rite before retiring can be very helpful. This is a true story.

I'd moved to Rio de Janeiro, Brazil, to do dissertation research and was spending a few weeks with a host family. The daughter and I shared a very small bedroom. A large window that was the size of a door, with the sill about waist high, looked up and out on the interior patio of the home. I did my bedtime meditation silently in the dark so I wouldn't wake my roommate. As I finished, I glanced out the open, screenless window from my bed and thought I saw one of the younger sons walking around the patio. I figured the boy couldn't sleep and was taking a walk. Wrong!

Suddenly he squatted by the window and peered in at us. As he crouched to jump into the room, in the moonlight I spied the steely glint of a knife in his hand. I shouted in Portuguese, "Get out of here now!"

The entire family jolted awake. The daughter began screaming. And the father, an army colonel, burst into the room with a loaded gun and shot off several rounds at the intruder, who hightailed it up the wall and over the roof. I hope your nightly protection ritual won't ever have to save your bacon as dramatically as it did mine, but you never know.

A User-Friendly Workspace

These days, many of us spend more time at work than home, or at least it seems that way. To make things worse, you may be obliged to cram yourself into a miniscule gray cubicle or computer station for several hours, only to endure a long commute home.

You can do tons of things to turn your workspace into a miniature haven away from home, whether you work in your own office, a cubicle, or at a computer station. I'm not promising the hours will pass like a brief interlude at the symphony. Still, a user-friendly, personalized space might tempt you, like the seven dwarves in *Snow White*, to "whistle while you work," which will certainly make you happier and more productive. Depending on how much room you have, you can try any of the following remedies.

Add a cozy, textured throw rug, a couple of postcards, a souvenir from a recent trip, or an adage on top of your computer. On my desk below my mainframe computer, I've a small bust of Charles Dickens, my literary hero, and a tiny statue of a track star mouse with a gold medal suspended from its neck. A plant or a framed photograph of an exotic destination will also go a long way toward making you feel at home in an institutionalized setting. Also bring something that reminds you of your hobby or other outside interest.

A colleague of mine whose two passions are horses and her family has displayed a couple photos of her husband and her daughter in attractive frames, as well as a snapshot of her and her horse winning a trophy. She's continued the theme with a horse blanket for a rug on the floor, two little equine figurines on the window ledge, and a mouse pad that's a comically grinning portrait of Mr. Ed, the talking horse. Her computer screensaver is a herd of wild horses grazing in a mountain meadow. What are your passions? Can you bring at least a couple of objects to represent them and remind you that you have a life outside of work?

Good, natural light is important for every employee's health and well-being. The Germans believe this is so important that they have legislated a "right to natural light" law, which requires that anybody working in an office should be able to see natural daylight through a window. This entitlement is considered so fundamental that businesses and corporations have been obliged to tear down inner walls, rearrange spaces, and build interior glass doors and windows so even the most subordinate employee sitting in a cubicle in the center of a room can see some of the outside world. A few American companies, such as Coors in Denver, have adopted this concept, but it has yet to catch on everywhere.

Even if the company where you work isn't as forward-looking as the Germans, you can chase away some of the shadows by adding a small lamp to your space. To create the illusion of being outdoors, take photos or collect postcards of beautiful exterior scenes and mount a collage on your cubicle or office wall.

While we're on the topic of photos, in a very unofficial survey of office spaces in my town, I've found that many people favor pics of pets over friends and relatives. Pets help lower their owners' blood pressure and make them feel relaxed and contented.

I don't know whether you dislike drinking from Styrofoam cups as much as I do, but if you do, I encourage you to add another comforting touch by keeping a china cup and saucer in your desk drawer. Next to them, store packets of your favorite sweetener, special teabags, premium cocoa, a tin of homemade chocolate chip cookies, or whatever little treat you like most. Remember that one of the five senses is taste, and here is where you can splurge.

For the sense of hearing, depending on the nature of your work, you might bring earbuds to listen to your music. Besides being relaxing, music energizes. Perhaps your songs will motivate you to complete that current project. Do make sure your tunes don't intrude on your coworkers. They're trying to create their own sanctuaries, too, as well as be productive.

Humor can invigorate a sacred space. One fellow I know who works in a travel agency keeps a bulletin board in his office with five or six cartoons having to do with the travel industry. Whenever he finds a hilarious joke, he replaces the oldest with the new one. Colleagues make a point of stopping by to view the latest witticism. The joke board helps maintain a light and breezy tone that lifts office morale.

A word of advice: keep your decorations within socially acceptable limits. While your office space provides a good place to express your interests, personal tastes, and perhaps even your cultural background, don't haul in a six-foot menorah or a hundred magazine foldouts of pinup girls. You're working in a professional environment, so your space should look professional and be respectful of others' feelings and beliefs.

Make Your Store a Sanctuary for All

This section is for store owners. It's entirely possible to extend the concept of a sanctuary to include your place of business. You're sure to draw more customers (always a good thing), and perhaps you'll also create a friendly environment for patrons, your staff, and you: a win-win situation for all! Here's what a friend of mine has done in her gift shop, Sweet Ruckus.

When setting up the establishment, Tania has paid attention to incorporating the five senses into the space. For sound, she plays music soft enough that people don't notice it consciously but loud enough to energize them. The type varies, but mostly, she says, "It's comfortable and cool, like lounge music, some jazz, and bossa nova. It's the kind of music for ambling through a place, smooth but not hurried, to generate a pleasant buzz." She starts the morning with mellow tunes and progresses to more uplifting sounds as the day progresses.

Tania believes that visuals and the quality of light and color are key to creating a congenial environment. For her, the lighting must be warm: "LEDs seem too blue and fluorescents are too sharp. This doesn't feel good subconsciously." In addition to the natural light flowing in from large plate-glass windows, she's added character with crystal chandeliers in different colors—blue, rose, violet, and green. The hanging crystals also add texture.

Speaking of texture, there's a children's corner displaying especially soft, sweet, and cuddly merchandise because, as Tania explains, "Children love to touch things, and texture is important to them." She also pays attention to texture in the other products she sells. For example, the high-quality paper products feel good, and the smooth leather purses for adults contrast nicely with the huggable toys.

As to the sense of smell, as an aromatherapist I was impressed by the light, sweet aromas permeating the store. Tania says she doesn't do anything on purpose because she doesn't want to overwhelm customers with aromas. Fragrances from products like soaps and bath bombs with their special scents, which she changes seasonally, disperse softly in the air. The fragrances change with the seasons—pumpkin spice in the fall, fir for winter, light and airy scents like lavender or sweet like hyacinth for spring, and sensuous jasmine and rose in summer.

One of the store's best features is how Tania displays the products and establishes a flowing movement of traffic through the space. In this, she follows some feng shui principles by positioning the merchandise and tables so there are no hard angles. The pathway through the aisles undulates from left to right and around with merchandise set at all levels—high, eye level, and low. This leaves plenty of room in the aisles so the customer doesn't feel boxed in.

Finally, Tania includes elements of nature that encourage people to feel they're coming into a friend's home. She's decorated with wood boughs and blooming flowers. The soft green paint on the walls is restful and makes a customer feel a bit like being on a nature walk. All in all, Tania has made Sweet Ruckus a beautiful, engaging place where customers can feel at ease and enjoy themselves. How will you design your store to achieve the same or similar purposes?

Mobile Sanctuaries

Any form of personal transportation, be it a car, truck, SUV, motorcycle, bicycle, or skateboard, constitutes a space where many feel we could use a bit more protection than airbags. Before you try the next remedy, check with the vehicle laws in your state. Most allow you to hang something from your rearview mirror, although there are a few exceptions. Mostly, law enforcement wants to make certain that what you put there doesn't obstruct your view when you're driving.

You've probably seen St. Christopher's medals, lucky dice, or mandalas suspended from motorists' rearview mirrors for protection. Some people affix a small statue of Buddha or a crucifix to the dashboard. The more practical may hang a small deodorizer cardboard tree or a scented sachet. To add a touch of humor to a hectic commute, my husband has glued a little rubber statue of Pink Panther to his dashboard with its hands covering its eyes. Others prefer to place an item in their car to show their ethnic origins or leisure pursuits. This wide range of decorations might include a shamrock, a small kachina doll, a Yoruba sigil, a miniature Big Ben, or something else that identifies the driver, such as a little bowling pin or tiny pair of skates. Some drivers write affirmations on paper and glue them to the dashboard.

The Charmed Chevy

We've all seen similar ways to personalize a vehicle, and perhaps you've done this yourself. But have you ever conceived of your vehicle as a means to move closer to heaven (without crashing it, of course)? As with many of the examples I've given throughout this book, I don't advocate that you appropriate anything that's not from your own ethnicity, but I hope the following story, although an extreme example, gets you thinking about what from your own cultural background you might want to incorporate into your vehicle.

There once was a man in Detroit who created quite a stir with the way he decorated his old Chevrolet. He glued hundreds of light bulbs, seashells, bits of shiny mirror, red reflectors, handless clocks, and a couple of chrome hubcaps, all sticking out at odd angles to the sides, back, and top of the car. Across the diameter of the hubcaps and wheels, he painted black lines that formed equal-armed crosses.

He festooned his vehicle in this way because in Vodou, his spiritual path, such symbols represent the journey of the soul through the cosmos to unite with the Creator. Two basic Creole-Congo concepts are evident in the Chevy's embellishments. The first is the dikenga sign, drawn as a cross in a circle. The cross symbolizes a crossroads or boundary between the mundane and spirit worlds. The circle symbolizes the soul's eternal cosmic orbit between birth, life, death, and rebirth. In the Congolese spiritual system, the vertical axis of the cross connects God above with the dead below, while the horizontal axis acts as a boundary between the living and the dead. Each arm of the cross mirrors the progress of the immortal soul on its eternal journey. Anything that interrupts this journey may lead to the soul's destruction. This is why the Chevy was marked with so many circular symbols like handless clocks and why the wheels included radiating crosses.

The other concept is called "flash and light," the power of light and movement to keep the spirit whole and moving so it avoids misadventure and destruction. Flash and light can also propel the soul on its path to glory and attract wealth on both the material and spiritual planes. The symbols used to express this idea on the car included light bulbs, tinfoil, bits of broken mirror, chrome hubcaps, sequins, and polished dimes and quarters.

What sort of protection symbol might you install in your vehicle?

Changing Homes

When you must pick up stakes and move away, especially if your new home is in another country, how do you reestablish your sanctuary? I base my comments on my years as an intercultural trainer and assessor, helping employees from the US and abroad relocate around the world because of their jobs. I'll talk about domestic moves later.

The prospect of living in a different, possibly exotic location can be thrilling. However, uprooting the family and moving to a place where even the most mundane activities like driving, purchasing and preparing food, or even taking a shower are totally different can be an unnerving experience. Living day in and day out in an environment where you're expected to think and act with normal adult speed and efficiency without knowing the rules of the game can lead to severe intercultural stress for you and your family. Behavioral psychologists call this phenomenon "culture shock."

One antidote to these challenges is to create a sanctuary in your new abode as soon as possible. I don't mean you should attempt to replicate your family's former physical environment in every detail. That would put you out of step with the new cultural environment. Let me give you an example.

When I lived in Wales, I met an American family living in a nearby village. When they moved, the wife insisted on bringing all her worldly goods from home, including pot-holders and dishtowels. It was as if she suspected the Welsh wouldn't have any. I shopped at the local craft market for tea towels and potholders that displayed Welsh vocabulary words accompanied by explanatory pictures. From these common household objects I learned colors, body parts, how to count to ten, and the meanings of some geographical terms, such as the words for hill, river, and waterfall, even if I couldn't pronounce them. And I had some lovely mementos and gifts from Wales to take back home when I returned.

Another American family lived near a US Army base and had friends purchase American products for them from the store on base. I remember the wife showing off gigantic box-es of cereal. The problem was that shelves in most Welsh cupboards are shorter and smaller than those in the United States, so they had to store their booty on the kitchen floor. Besides that inconvenience, they ended up missing out on trying many tasty regional products. Sadly, these people had such an unhappy experience that they left before the term of their assignment was over.

To establish a haven abroad, I recommend taking along some familiar things—your son's preferred board game, your daughter's beloved doll, your husband's favorite sci-fi nov-els, your own comfortable pillow. Familiar touches will evoke fond memories and buck you up when you're feeling frus-trated, confused, or homesick. At the same time, don't take anything you'd hate to lose. Don't take the precious family jewels or your best china.

Before you depart, make it a family project to collect and mount photographs in an album. I think a physical album rather than your phone or a computer disc is the best way to go. Leafing through an actual album, being able to point to and touch each picture, makes for a tangible, durable memory experience. Include photos of family, friends, pets, your house, place of worship, community center, and local landscapes. Albums perform double duty. You can thumb through them when you're feeling blue and show them to friends in the new culture when describing your origins and background. You never know when you'll be asked to speak to some group, such as a community center, house of worship, or school.

Before leaving, buy a glossy picture book that depicts where you come from. Since I live in the Rocky Mountain West, I've taken along books that display the beauties of the High Country, a regional cookbook, tales of the Old West, Native American traditions, Denver, and photos of homesteaders' quilts. Before you return to the US, give the books to a friend's child as mementos.

To facilitate the adaptation process to the new culture, incorporate something from the host environment into your home. It could be something as simple and inexpensive as a hand-embroidered blouse or a handsome straw basket woven by a local craftsperson. For me in Wales, it was a large Welsh lovespoon carved from a single piece of sycamore and meant to hang in the home to confer fertility and good luck on the family.

While in Rio de Janeiro, I acquired a turquoise parakeet. Birds are popular choices for pets among Brazilians, and this gave me some conversational currency to exchange with my friends and neighbors—especially since my bird was trilingual. He could say "pretty bird" in English, Portuguese, and Spanish! When I left, I gave my parakeet to a friend, who adores it to this day.

I'll never forget the apartment of a cultural attaché I knew in Brasília, the capital of Brazil. This diplomat had covered one of her dining room walls from ceiling to floor with primitive paintings bursting with color. Whenever she traveled around the country, she visited local craft fairs. She chose pictures that depicted some aspect of Brazilian rural or domestic life: rubber collectors in the Amazon; white-clad, turbaned women dancing at a festival in the Northeast; coffee pickers in the fields of the South; vendors hawking sweets associated with the deities of the Afro-Brazilian pantheon at the beach. The quality of the artwork varied, but what mattered most was that she had assembled a vibrant, breathing tribute to Brazil's cultural heritage. She could return home with her living wall and reassemble it as an elegant and significant personal memory of her time abroad.

Even if you're planning a domestic move, you can help smooth the transition by adapting many of the abovementioned tips to fit your individual circumstances. The possibilities are as infinite as your imagination.

Living on a Budget

Nowadays, many employees who transfer either domestically or abroad get paid by their employers—sometimes handsomely—to relocate. As an adult, I've lived in six countries and made eighteen domestic moves, and never did anybody pay for my expenses, give me a budget, or help me settle in. So I feel I can say with confidence that I am qualified to advise about how to relocate and live on a budget. For those of you in the same boat, here are some tips.

It almost goes without saying that you should travel light. Nothing is more discouraging and exhausting than having to lug around loads of personal possessions. Have faith that with a bit of ingenuity, all—well, most all—will be provided.

Renting a place that's already furnished will cut down hugely on moving expenses. In Europe and most of Latin America (I haven't lived in other regions, so I don't know about Asia, Africa, or the Middle East, for example), the landlord usually supplies basic kitchenware—plates, cups, silverware, pots and pans, etc. Make an inventory when you move in because your landlord will do the same when you leave, and you don't want to be stuck with paying for something you didn't break or that was taken by a previous tenant. If you're relocating solo, consider finding a roommate or two to share expenses.

I've moved to unfurnished digs three times. My studio in Providence, Rhode Island, had only a mattress on the floor and a rickety bedside table, and in Rio there wasn't even a refrigerator in the apartment. What did I do? I made friends, and these very kind people lent me the basics for what I needed to live. In succeeding years I've returned the favor by supplying some of my friends with items they needed when they came to live in my town.

Take a hint from chapter 9 on downsizing, only do it in reverse: shop at Goodwill and other charity stores, resale emporiums, flea markets, Facebook Marketplace, Etsy Vintage, yard sales (they're called "boot sales" in the United Kingdom), etc., to furnish your place. If you're living abroad, your local consulate or embassy will keep lists of items, both large and small, that expatriates want to sell as they're leaving to go back home. You can get incredible deals there.

Be creative with what you buy. I once purchased a small and pretty beat-up wooden table for my kitchenette. I sanded out the nicks and scrapes and painted it a solid color, later adding a design. As far as creativity goes, apply a suggestion from chapter 10 on living in small spaces and buy multipurpose furnishings. For example, an inexpensive day bed will double as a couch. And of course, there's always the instant bookcase: cement blocks and boards. In a pinch, you can use a steamer trunk for a coffee table and a suitcase or two piled on top of each other for an end table. An inexpensive folding card table and chairs can serve you well as a dining table. This is what I used in my various graduate school apartments, and I was still eating off the same table twelve years later in my first house. I simply covered it with a pretty tablecloth and nobody knew the difference.

As for decoration, use your ingenuity. When I moved to Rio, I quickly learned an amazing fact: plants grow fast in the tropics. If I took a cutting from a planter on the sidewalk and stuck it into an empty yogurt cup filled with water, the cutting miraculously took root overnight. I didn't have much furniture when I lived in Brazil, but I sure had an apartment full of flourishing greenery.

And the pretty scarf you may have brought from home or picked up at a craft fair will look elegant when used to cover a table that has seen better days.

Remember when I talked about refrigerator art in chapter 7? You can extend this concept to your walls. Make your own drawings or paintings on good paper or have your children make collages and tack them to the walls.

One thing to not skimp on is lamps. This is the voice of experience talking, and this voice says that I've never moved to a place with enough lighting. Buy some small, cheap table lamps and set them around your abode. They'll go a long way toward filling the place with good cheer.

Turkman Weavings

What if the place where you live doesn't allow for the amenity of a personal haven? What if you never stay in one location long enough to establish a rapport with anyone or anything? What if you are a nomad? How do you forge a personal sanctuary?

For centuries, women of the Turkman culture, a nomadic tribe of Central Asia, have used their expertise as weavers to convey their individuality and cultural identity. Women learn to weave and embroider everything from towels to pillows and prayer rugs. They also create exquisite flat-woven kilims to cover the floors of their tents.

The patterns and symbols they weave into the rugs, such as images of birds, wild animals, and geometrical designs, may describe their family or clan associations. Personal hopes, dreams, disappointments, and accomplishments, such as longing for a husband, pride in birthing a son, agony over the loss of a child, or contentment in a long-lasting friendship, are also sewn into the designs. Through her constructions, a weaver strives to create an artifact that will last throughout her life and perhaps for generations beyond as a testament to her cultural identity.

Here's a takeaway from Turkman weavings. If you're handy with a needle, you can make a needlepoint or crewelwork sampler of your own design to reflect your feelings. If you have artistic talent, how about painting a picture to hang on your sanctuary wall? We'll explore more thoroughly the topic of cultural identity in the next chapter.

fourteen

A Sanctuary to Express Your Cultural Identity

You may not be contemplating an international move to an exotic location, as we talked about in the last chapter, yet you yearn to travel, either internationally or domestically. Or, like many of us, maybe you're an armchair traveler. Moreover, after reading about what people from other cultures have done to create their havens, you may want to make a sanctuary that reflects your own cultural identity. For those who fit any of these categories, this chapter provides information on how to accomplish that goal. It also addresses sanctuaries worldwide that may inspire you to recombine what you learn from them synergistically into your own haven.

First things first: What is culture, and what does it mean to belong to one? Simply put, culture is a way of life. It is a set of values, attitudes, habits, beliefs, symbols, and behaviors of a group of people that they generally accept and pass along from one generation to the next. A person's culture is influenced by ethnicity, geography, religion, social class, generation, and gender, among other factors. Culture manifests in customs, traditions, music, ways of dressing, objects held in esteem, artistic expression, and much more. Your culture is important to you because it helps define your self-conception and self-perception and links you to a distinct social group or groups.

To be able to incorporate your personal culture into your sanctuary, you might want to learn more about your cultural background. You may think you know all about this, but once you start researching, some surprising answers may reveal themselves.

The first place to go to explore your roots is to your parents and other relatives, especially elders. Ask them about stories they heard from their older relatives. See what kinds of artifacts they keep around to remind them of the past. They may share old photos and photo albums with you that may have additional information written on them. They may also remember traditions they heard about but that nobody in the family practices anymore. The information they offer is valuable, but not infallible. Unbeknownst to them, their ethnicity may be wholly or in part different from what they suppose.

The next step is to verify what you've been told. Research historical records and other public information sites, which are usually free. Comb through records kept at the Library of Congress, National Archives and Records, Archives.com,

Heritage Quest Online, and other sites. Check census records for family history, newspaper articles about them such as obituaries, passenger lists from immigration ports of entry, and naturalization papers.

To delve deeper into genealogy, check out Ancestry.com, which is the world's largest online family history resource. Taking DNA tests will uncover your ancestral roots, show migration paths, and add depth to your family history. Eventually, you will put together a cultural mosaic that shows who you are and which parts of your heritage you wish to celebrate in your sanctuary.

If you feel you want to add something more, review some of the many different traditions from other cultures presented in this book. You don't need to copy any of these unique customs to derive some benefit from them. You might even find some similarities with customs from your own background that you may have forgotten. For example, if you are of Scandinavian or Japanese descent, the Native American sweat lodge might prompt you to reinstitute the custom of taking a sauna. Who knows? You may even construct one in your home.

Here's another example: Americans and other English-speaking people are well-known for the high value we place on privacy. In fact, many other languages don't even have a term to express this value and have had to borrow the English word to describe the concept. But as it turns out, we're not the only people with this attitude. For the Japanese, private space is always in short supply. In the past, families lived jammed into small houses with walls made from boards and rice paper that abutted their neighbors' literally paper-thin walls. Even today, when much of the urban population dwells in concrete apartment blocks, private space continues to be an issue for the privacy-craving Japanese.

People have devised various ways to respect each other's privacy. Avoiding eye contact, for instance, signals that a person wants to be left alone. Meditation is also greatly esteemed, and the Japanese are accustomed to practicing it in the bath or while taking walks in nature. In these places they feel free to withdraw from society and invite inner peace. As a takeaway, I suggest you re-read the chapter on bathrooms, viewing it through your own cultural lens. What can you do in your bathroom haven that may be part of your own cultural tradition?

A Bottle Tree to Heal Souls

Remember the story about the charmed Chevy? Another protection symbol that Vodou practitioners use is a bottle tree. They suspend colored glass bottles or plastic bottles filled with colored water from a dead or living tree in their yard. The bottles represent containment of negative energy. The colored glass also catches the light, replicating the flash and light that propels the soul to heaven. By decorating a bottle tree, the dweller constructs a sacred space that protects the home, facilitates the journey of the soul, and also communicates a unique cultural heritage to the world. Here is what a group of friends did to adapt this idea for healing.

Having learned about the power of the bottle tree from African-American traditions, after Hurricane Katrina hit New Orleans, a group of friends—two of them African-American Vodou practitioners—decided to exercise this concept to aid the souls of the dead who so rapidly and violently were wrenched from earth. We created a bottle tree in the mountain ash at our side yard, hanging colorful miniature liqueur bottles from the branches. Then we stood in a circle around the tree, chanted a prayer for the victims, and concentrated on propelling them toward the light and heaven. A year later, we unhooked the bottles, dug a hole in the ground below the tree, and emptied the bottles' contents into it with a final prayer for the souls who had moved on.

Heritage Travel and
Sacred Sites of the World

Once you've established your cultural identity and incorporated customs and traditions into your sanctuary, there's more you can do to enhance your experience. Google "heritage tours" and you'll find several sites dedicated to providing tours for people who wish to travel to their places of origin to explore their roots. You can go as a group or hire a private guide.

If you enjoy traveling and value experiences, I recommend taking a trip to a world-famous sacred site. In addition to learning why it is considered blessed, you may bring back ideas on how to incorporate some of the sacredness into your own haven.

The concept of a group of sacred sites that have been revered throughout the ages is not new. A catalog of the seven wonders of the ancient Western world was drawn up long ago during the Middle Ages. In those days, gigantic manmade constructions were honored because they reflected humans' ability to control nature by engineering changes in the landscape. These days, the idea of what constitutes a world wonder has changed. Besides showing human constructions, lists now include locations in nature, some of them on continents not much explored in ancient times, such as Asia, Africa, and the Americas. Millions of tourists undertake long and sometimes arduous pilgrimages to these spots in much the same way people did in times gone by.

Here is a top ten list that includes both natural wonders and manmade achievements:

1. The Great Pyramid at Giza, Egypt
2. The Grand Canyon, Arizona
3. The Great Wall, China
4. The Taj Mahal, India
5. The Serengeti Migration, Africa
6. Machu Picchu, Peru
7. The Roman Coliseum, Italy
8. Antarctica
9. Amazon Rainforest, South America
10. Iguaçu Falls, South America

I've chosen four of my favorite natural sites to share here. I hope you can visit these spectacular places and bring back some amazing experiences and ideas for your sanctuary at home. Of course, you'll want to select sites depending on your interests and travel budget, and don't worry if you can't afford the time or the money to travel. Later in the chapter, I'll address sanctuaries you can find closer to home.

Iguaçu Falls (A Foz de Iguaçu): Raw Power of Nature

The first on my list of beloved sites is one of the top ten. I arrived at the falls by car after journeying deep into the tropical interior of Brazil to where it borders with Argentina and Paraguay. An untold number of people have made this pilgrimage to observe, feel, hear, smell, and perhaps even taste the astounding power of water from 275 cascades that plunge 269 feet into the Iguaçu River at the average rate of 1.2 million cubic meters per second. The Guaraní Indians named the falls "Great Water," and they are great, indeed!

Trek through semi-deciduous and tropical woods bursting with richly varied flora and fauna to the cascade called *Garganta do Diabo* ("devil's throat"), an elongated horseshoe of a cascade as tall as a twenty-four-story building. It offers extraordinary views of both the falls and a forest of pines, palms, bamboos, trailing vines, and colorful orchids and begonias that stretches as far as the eye can see. The water's thunderous roar takes your breath away. It's impossible not to be profoundly moved by such splendid scenery that so dramatically manifests the raw power of the element.

Tips and Takeaways: *I recommend hiring a guide who will ensure that you view the falls from their most spectacular and safe vantage point. Your guide will explain a lot about the area, and if you're looking for a place to sit in undisturbed meditation, this expert will take you to an appropriate spot. You might also want to contemplate something to do on a very small scale with a water feature in your sanctuary back home. To recapture some of Iguaçu's grandeur, you could set up a tabletop fountain surrounded by miniature tropical indoor plants and ferns.*

Stonehenge and Avebury: Ancient Ingenuity

Ancient people, who were more attuned to nature than we are today, believed that these forces vibrated most strongly in certain places. They created sanctuaries at those locations, often constructing stone circles around them to honor nature and the gods they imagined represented it. Stonehenge, located on the Salisbury Plain in Wiltshire, England, and nearby Avebury provide two stellar examples. Stonehenge, the most famous, was constructed during the Bronze Age, three thousand years ago.

It began as an earthwork enclosure where prehistoric people buried their dead. Over time, worshippers added at least 83 stones, probably more. The sarsen stones (large sandstone blocks) are the largest. Each one stands 13 feet high and 7 feet wide and weighs 25 tons. These enormous rocks were toted from a location 20 miles distant. The smaller yet still substantial bluestones, so named for their blueish tint, were transported from Wales, even farther away, probably by boat.

The worshippers arranged the stones in two concentric rings. It has been posited that the outer ring may represent the twelve astrological signs and the inner ring exemplifies the lunar months and cycles. The circles also measure the sun's position at the solstices, a crucial point to prehistoric people, who may have believed that without the rituals conducted there, the sun might never return after winter to warm the earth.

Avebury, less well known to tourists but significant to archaeologists, consists of three circles that cover twenty-eight acres bounded by a deep ditch. Several segments of the circles have disappeared because stones were used to construct the buildings in Avebury village. Nevertheless, enough of the original structures remain to show that this was an exceptional sacred place in constant use from the Neolithic to the Bronze Age.

Two avenues lined with standing stones laid out in an undulating pattern have led some researchers to theorize they mimic the movements of snakes and that a cult revolving around serpent worship once was active there. During those times, serpents were believed to increase fertility in humans, restore youth, and confer immortality on their worshippers, so it's possible that the avenues were used for fertility rites. On the other hand, critics point out that not many snakes have ever thrived in England. Perhaps their relative rarity helped make these reptiles so worshipped. A few researchers now think the undulations represent water, an element that often is associated with fertility.

At both Stonehenge and Avebury, eminent dowsers like Paul Devereux and Tom Graves have experienced energy vibrations emanating from the megaliths. A dowser is a person who uses a forked stick to find well water and buried treasure and also to locate energy centers in the ground. These investigators and others feel a tingling sensation like an electrical charge pass through their hands and arms when they touch the stones. They also sometimes receive the impression that the rocks move, even though they know the stones have not shifted position.

As in feng shui, which uses shapes to direct the flow of chi, dowsers believe stones of different shapes can both retain and emit energy. Perhaps what they experience when touching the stones is two thousand years of contained energy that humans stored in them long ago. What an exhilarating sensation!

> TIPS AND TAKEAWAYS: *Unless you're an avid sun worshipper, try to give Stonehenge a skip on the summer solstice. If you must, go at the winter solstice, when the usually cold, wet, and windy weather discourages tourists. Also, Avebury is less frequented than Stonehenge. See if you can feel energy emanating from the stones at Avebury. If you can, you might want to visit a rock shop and buy a couple of small stones that speak to you in a similar way. Take them back to your haven to energize your life.*

Cliff Dwellers of Mesa Verde:
A Mysterious and Exquisite Location

Recently I revisited Mesa Verde in the Four Corners area of southwest Colorado near the town of Durango. This site also features stones, but these rocks were used by the cliff-dwelling Anasazi Indians to build homes and storage areas in the recesses of canyon walls. More than four thousand sites in this area, now a Ute reservation, are under the protection of Mesa Verde National Park.

The Anasazi built and inhabited these cliffs for a short time between 1200 and 1300 CE. The choice of location is puzzling because more appropriate, previously settled terrain exists nearby. Perplexing to many is the fact the community was abandoned after less than a century. It has been proposed that the Anasazi either were driven out by invaders or, more probably, left the region under the specter of drought. However, our guide—who was raised in the area and who is half Indian (he prefers this term)—insisted there's no mystery to it. He maintained, "When it's time for the people to go, they simply leave. Everything not necessary for the journey stays there to honor and feed Mother Earth."

The amazing dwellings are strung out seemingly at random around the cliffs and range in size from a single cubicle to the Cliff Palace boasting 217 rooms. The builders fitted the residences into natural alcoves that protected them from the ravages of weather and erosion, so they have stayed in relatively good condition. From afar, you might think the community still teems with life.

The masonry work varies from rough sandstone construction to well-shaped stones. Many rooms are plastered on the inside and decorated with painted designs. From the artifacts found around the sites, it's obvious that the Anasazi were accomplished at using stone, wood, and copper tools, and were expert pottery and basketry craftspeople. This was, indeed, an advanced civilization.

For me, the most salient feature of the location is its perfectly silent, mysterious ambience. When I explore these dwellings located below a high, dry plateau and surrounded by piñon trees, juniper, serviceberries, and sagebrush, I'm entranced by the sophisticated but short-lived culture that made a lasting impression on the landscape. I'm also overcome by a profound sense of sadness and nostalgia for a way of life long extinct that never will return to this earth.

TIPS AND TAKEAWAYS: *Avoid crowds by planning your trip there during the off season (October–early May). You'll get more out of the experience if you hire a guide. Frank Miller of Mountain Waters Rafting and Adventure is a goldmine of information, expounding on everything from the geology, geography, and botany of the region to the people who have inhabited it. He makes the area come alive, as if you were seeing a panoramic march of history rise up before your eyes. As a bonus, his wife, whose ancestors were among the first Spanish people to settle the region, provides a lunch featuring regional food. There are plenty of locations for you to sit and meditate or simply drink in your surroundings. The area is so silent, without a hint of noise or lights from outside civilization, that you almost can't be disturbed. When you leave, try to take that feeling of complete silence within a timeless universe back home to your sanctuary.*

Great Barrier Reef: World Wonder in Jeopardy

Off the northeast coast of Queensland, Australia, lies a World Heritage Site that CNN has called one of the seven natural wonders of the world. I've decided to end this personal inventory with perhaps the most extraordinary outdoor sanctuary of all, yet one in extreme peril.

The Great Barrier Reef can only be described using superlatives. It is the world's largest coral reef system and one of the world's largest living structures, so big it can be seen from space. It is comprised of 2,900 individual reefs that stretch for 1,700 miles along the coast. This complex of reefs has always been important to the Aboriginal Australian and Torres Strait Islander people as a cultural and spiritual center. In recent times it has become a popular destination for eco-tourists, snorkelers, and scuba divers. The reef is a vital natural wonder because of the diverse, vulnerable, and endangered life it shelters and supports.

The following statistics give an idea of how key the reef is to sustaining life in the region and on the planet. Here you will find 6 species of sea turtles, 1,500 fish species as well as the dwarf minke whale and the Indo-Pacific humpback whale mammals, 17 species of sea snakes, and 125 species of sharks, as well as scores of species of chimaera, skates, and stingrays. In the nearby saltwater marshes, among the sea grasses, live several species of crocodile. As if that weren't enough, there are 5,000 species of mollusks and 9 of seahorses. Two hundred fifteen bird species nest or roost there, and 1.4 to 1.7 million birds also breed on the reef. The reef also nourishes 2,195 known plant species and over 500 different algae and seaweeds, not to mention the 400 actual coral species for which it is renowned.

So why is this natural marvel in jeopardy? Not surprisingly, the reef is under attack by a myriad of environmental and human threats. Climate change, pollution, and the proliferation of crown-of-thorns starfish that prey on coral polyps are the chief culprits.

Coral polyps—tiny animals that consume algae—are literally in hot water. Normally, they form colonies and build colorful scaffolding to live in, which forms a reef. When the seawater gets too warm, the algae, the corals' food source, produce a toxin. The corals expel the toxin, turning white or "bleaching" in self-defense. If they expel too much toxin, they starve to death or are killed off by disease and crown-of-thorns starfish. Two-thirds of the once-pristine northern reefs are now destroyed.

As to pollution, burning fossil fuels leads to increased greenhouse gasses that heat the sea and worsen the situation for the corals. Another type of pollution comes from tourism. Besides the more than two million ecotourists who visit the region yearly, ironically upsetting the delicate balance of nature they claim to support, the tourism industry builds permanent platforms so sightseers can view the splendor and scuba divers can get a diving platform. Birds land on the platforms and leave excrement that washes into the sea, adding to waters already polluted from fertilizer and pesticide runoff from farms located on nearby land.

Although the area is not ideally suited for a shipping lane, it is marginally better than some nearby routes. As a result, there has been a noted uptick in traffic and in shipping vessel accidents. Oil spills are common, and more than 1,600 wrecks have occurred. To add insult to injury, human hunters prey upon the slow-moving, inoffensive dugong (similar to a manatee) and the green sea turtle, both of which are now endangered.

I have chosen the Great Barrier Reef as my final world sanctuary to draw attention to its plight. My hope is to spur readers to take action and support rehabilitation efforts in this region.

TIPS AND TAKEAWAYS: *The reef is such a popular destination that you'll have no trouble booking a tour there, especially if you're into scuba diving or snorkeling. However, please be especially respectful of this very delicate ecosystem that may not be with us much longer. In my opinion, the best thing you can do as a takeaway is to support the Ocean Conservancy and other organizations dedicated to preserving this sacred space that is vital to earth's survival.*

Sacred Sites Close to Home

To honor your heritage as well as to visit sacred sites, you don't need to travel halfway around the globe; you can probably discover some in your own neighborhood. To do this, find others who share your background. They could be of the same ethnic heritage or share similar interests. As to interests, I've found a couple of friends in my town who come from Detroit, the city where I grew up. We love getting together and exchanging stories about the old stomping ground. Go online and look for people who attended the same schools as you. Friends from the past may emerge. I attended a high school reunion a couple of years ago, and two of my buddies from elementary and middle school are now chatting online with me regularly. One even contributed the vegan smoothie recipe to this book.

As to your cultural heritage, I urge you to go online and seek out social clubs or associations of people from your ethnic origin. If you can't find anybody that way, look for talks to attend where people of your background might gather. For example, if you are Italian, you might see a public lecture advertised about Italian archeology. Attend the talk and see who else is there. Be sure to socialize afterward. Taking a class on a subject that involves your ethnic roots may work the same way. French cuisine, Australian winetasting, or Japanese calligraphy could lead to forging new relationships with people of your ethnicity. At the very least, you'll learn something about your ancestors' contributions to society to incorporate into your sanctuary. Although I'm not Italian, I hope to go to Italy next fall. So I've been attending an Italian circle where people meet at a nearby Tuscan restaurant to eat and practice the language. I'm learning so much from this group about Italian culture as well as the language.

As to finding sacred spaces in your neighborhood, I suggest you visit a nearby park. Walking around my town, I've recently found two sacred spaces I had no idea existed. The first is an outdoor maze at a church just eight blocks from my house. A sign encourages people to trace the circular paths to the middle while reading the aphorisms and quotes from scripture etched into the stones. When you're through the maze, the church has provided a shady bench to sit in contemplation for as long as you want.

I literally ran across the second sacred site while jogging around my hometown. It's a perfect example of a temporary outdoor altar that has surfaced seemingly of its own accord. Boulder Creek runs from twenty miles west in the mountains through the center of the city and from there on to the Eastern Plains. A spontaneous altar has sprung up on a pylon near downtown that sustains a bridge across the creek. On the flat top of the eight-inch square surface, people leave little offerings. They may be as simple as a pretty stone, a flower, or a couple of feathers. Sometimes more valuable objects appear like necklaces, rings, statuettes, bits of embroidery, or even a prayer on a paper scroll.

The altar is ever-changing. Items appear and disappear. One thing is for certain: this mutable altar persists in all seasons, all weather, and in every month for at least the last five years. In my opinion, this community altar reinforces the belief that spirituality comes in all shapes and sizes, and sometimes people feel the need to express their devotion outside in nature. This is something that unites the human family, no matter the individual's spiritual path.

Somebody once asked me how I knew a site was sacred. In the cases of the famous ones, so many people have believed this to be true over so many years, instilling the sites with their faith and acceptance, that if they weren't sacred places before, they're sure to be now. Moreover, you can apply the first concepts outlined in this book—that is, to use your five senses. What can you see, feel, smell, hear, and even taste about the location? Trust your intuition. If you resonate with the place, then it is sacred, at least to you.

Afterword

Coming Home

I recently attended an exhibit at the University of Colorado Art Museum. The works consisted mainly of photographs taken by the likes of Ansel Adams, Joseph David, Lawrence McFarland, and the Hudson River School. They explored the theme of thoughts, feelings, and views about the meaning of home from multiple perspectives. Photos of earth from 240,000 miles away, landscapes, house interiors, and people living in their homes showed how home is imagined both as a collective memory and in a private sense as individual experiences. The exhibit revealed how home is conceived as both a real and fantastical space. Besides the evocative imagery, the curators had erected a large bulletin board. Next to it they placed a table with a stack of three-by-five cards, tacks, and pencils for visitors to express what home meant to them and display their thoughts on the board anonymously.

Reading the cards, I found certain key themes repeated. Sentiments included the idea that home is not necessarily a place, more a feeling of security, healing, and sanctuary. Taking center stage were family, friends, and pets. (More respondents referred to pets than people.) Many mentioned that their notion of home is a place of love, laughter, and freedom from responsibility—a nonjudgmental environment. A place of comfort was highlighted, often along with mention of favorite foods. Others wrote of home as where they could revisit fond memories and find renewal and self-realization. Some of my favorite quotes were:

> "Home is not a location but wherever those I love are walking."

> "Home feels like being under a warm blanket in a cold room."

> "Home is a place of velvety contentment."

> "Home is where I don't have to wear pants."

> "Home is when and where you can forget about the past and the future. When you're just being, here and now."

An especially creative person wrote that home was "(H)ealing (O)f (M)y (E)ntire being."

One of the most insightful comments, and one which I wish to leave you with as you journey toward forging your personal sanctuary, read "Home is what you make of it."

I hope this book has given you ideas on how to continue your spiritual journey. I wish you well in your endeavors to create your own sanctuary where you will find some peace. May your sanctuaries shine on!

Appendix

This appendix contains information designed to help enhance your sanctuary experience. Here you will find details on traditional meanings for botanicals, flowers, gemstones, numbers, totems, and trees, as well as key words about how to use them for meditation. Since the explanations are necessarily brief, you may want to consider the topics that interest you as a guide for doing further research on your own. Again, if you have pets or children, check for toxicity before incorporating any of these plants into your home and garden decorating scheme.

Botanicals

African Violet (*Saintpaulia* genus). If you're fond of cheerful indoor blossoms, this little plant from Tanzania and Kenya is right for you. Among the thousands of existing cultivars (a cultivar is a plant variety that has been produced in cultivation by selective breeding), the most admired ones sport neat rosettes of purple or pink blossoms atop furry green leaves. This violet is something of a diva in that it requires a fair amount of care. Wait until the soil dries to water it, and then only add tepid moisture from the bottom. African violets also require 10–14 hours of light and a year-round temperature of 65–80 degrees. On the other hand, this fairly compact plant fits nicely on a shelf or in a terrarium and only needs repotting once a year. Meditate on the African violet to open your third eye to spirituality and insights, balance your personality, perform moon magic, and become more fluid and adaptable.

Aloe Vera (*Aloe vera* genus). This succulent perennial of the lily family is native to the West Indies, where it blooms all year long. It's a fashionable houseplant in northern climes and is readily available at florist shops, nurseries, and even at the supermarket. Although the plant is edible, some varieties are extremely bitter. Aloe gel, which comes from the leaf, conditions hair and soothes sunburn, cuts, and scrapes. As to spiritual associations, ancient Egyptians hung aloe from their doorways as a sign the dweller had made a religious pilgrimage. This botanical symbolizes love and the strong bonds between friends and family. Both make excellent meditation topics.

Amaryllis (*Hippeastrum* genus). The large bulbs of this indoor plant make ideal house gifts for the winter holidays. Two to four large trumpet-shaped blooms in red, pink, or white grow on long spikes. Plant your bulb so one-third of it extends above the soil and water sparingly until it flowers, then move it to a sunny location; the flowers last a long time. Meditate on amaryllis to gain self-confidence and to not become too prideful.

Angelica (*Angelica archangelica*). A perennial of the carrot family, angelica flourishes in cool climates, where the thick stem can grow as tall as a small tree. It prefers partial shade and rich, moist, slightly acidic soil. The umbrella-like flowers are greenish-white and emit a delicious, honey-like scent. All parts of the plant are used in cooking and herbal medicine. The taste of the stalk is reminiscent of celery. Candied stalks make a treat.

In herbal medicine angelica can increase the circulation when the body needs an extra push. An infusion of the seeds helps relieve intestinal gas. The tea decocted from the root is an aromatic stimulant and tonic that combats nausea, coughs, colds, and urinary tract infections.

Legend has it that angelica was revealed to humanity by the Archangel Michael, hence the scientific name for the plant. In ancient times this herb was considered a remedy against contagious diseases, poisons, and plague, and was said to neutralize evil. In the language of flowers, this plant symbolizes inspiration, which makes it a good plant to contemplate during meditation. Since angelica can grow very tall and has thick stems, it can be thought of as an indoor meditation tree.

Bee Balm (*Monarda* genus). Also known as bergamot, monarda, and Oswego tea, bee balm is a perennial of the mint family. Like most mints, it grows one to three feet, tends to spread horizontally via its root system, and enjoys sun to partial shade and moist, acidic soil. There are over 140 varieties of this plant. Most have two-lipped scarlet, pink, violet, or white blossoms. The parts used to make tea or herbal medicine are the leaves and flowers. The taste is citrus-minty with a hint of pepper. If you want to approximate the taste of Earl Grey tea by preparing your own, add some of the leaves to China black or Darjeeling. Bee balm is an antidepressant. The tea is also good for uterine and intestinal cramps, joint pain, and fluid retention. Meditate on bee balm for protection and to climb out of a rut.

Borage (*Borago officinalis*). Although borage is an annual, it reseeds itself so readily that it can be considered a perennial. This outdoor plant grows from one to three feet, where it enjoys sun or partial shade and fairly dry, average soil. The flowers, which grow in nodding clusters, resemble little blue stars and attract swarms of bees. The parts used are the leaves and flowers. The leaves provide an interesting salad green with a cool, cucumber-like taste. When consumed as a tea, this herb produces perspiration that helps the body eliminate toxins. Meditate on borage to lift your spirits and strengthen your resolve.

Boston Fern (*Nephrolepis exaltada 'Bostoniensis'*). This indoor fern, also known as the sword fern, is so named for the shape of its gracefully arching, wavy fronds. A lush Boston fern in a hanging basket will lend a tropical air to your environment. It tolerates poor light but requires high humidity. This fern is nontoxic to pets and people, unlike its cousin the asparagus fern, and helps remove many pollutants from the air. Meditate on Boston fern to raise consciousness through life experience, acquire ancient knowledge, and improve health.

Clover (*Trifolium pratense*). The two kinds of clover have white or red blossoms. Both are bee magnets. You may find white clover invading your grass; I consider it a weed. On the other hand, the perennial red clover (whose blossoms are pinkish or purple, not red) is the kind used in herbal medicine and for brewing tea. It also makes a good soil improvement crop and fodder. This plant grows up to two feet and likes sun and average soil. The grassy-smelling flower heads taste sweet and some of the best honey is produced from them. Fertilize with organics.

In herbal medicine red clover helps balance the female reproductive system and is beneficial in cases of bronchial congestion and whooping cough because it is an antispasmodic. According to folklore traditions, sprinkling clover water on the doorstep of your store or home attracts business and prosperity. The four-leafed clover is considered a good luck charm, while the three-leafed variety symbolizes the Holy Trinity, hence protection against evil and negativity. Meditate on clover for success, faithfulness, and protection.

Fennel (*Foeniculum vulgare*). Fennel is a three-foot umbelliferous kitchen garden perennial that looks and tastes like a combination of dill, licorice, and anise. If you plant it outside, pick the seeds before they have time to scatter unless you want to raise scores of little fennel babies. Fennel flavors fish, salads, and soups. If you're on a diet, they say you can chew the seeds to suppress your appetite. Personally, I haven't noticed that this works, but fennel does sweeten the breath.

This herb supports good digestion and milk production in lactating women.

In medieval times people believed that if they blocked their keyholes with fennel, the herb would discourage ghosts from entering the house. At least a draft wouldn't make it through the keyhole! Ancient folks also thought that by consuming this herb, they gained strength, courage, and longevity. Therefore, you can meditate on a small dish full of fennel seeds to gain strength and courage. Afterward, chew on a couple seeds to sweeten your breath.

Fig (*Ficus carica*). Many kinds of fig trees, shrubs, and vines abound. Some produce figs; others don't. Edible dwarf figs, some of which can winter over in cold climates if carefully mulched, are my favorites. 'Little Ruby' and 'Brown Turkey' figs make especially lovely small indoor trees. Not only do they provide delicious fruit, they also remove most air pollutants. The dwarfs reach six to eight feet with a six-foot span and should be kept in a sunny window.

Remove the figs' peels and seeds and combine with apple juice, ice cream, or milk for a to-die-for smoothie; that is, if you can refrain from popping them into your mouth before they make it into the blender! Although figs are high in calories for their small size, they are touted as appetite suppressants. Scientists have discovered a component in the leaves called benzaldehyde, which has since been incorporated into some cancer-fighting drugs.

Two common figs that may not produce fruit but which have become standard office and contemporary-style apartment greenery are the fiddle-leaf fig (*F. lyrata*) and the weeping fig (*F. benjamina*). Both fill an empty corner nicely or make a statement in an entryway. These varieties have acquired a bad reputation for leaf drop, but this is because they often suffer from shocking neglect. Plant your fig in well-drained soil, water when it appears dry, and shelter it from cold drafts. Try not to move it once it is in its permanent home, and wipe the rich, green-colored leaves clean from dust every once in a while. If you do these things, your fig will reward you with years of service. To keep your tree from growing taller than six feet, trim the root ball by up to 20 percent every four to six months.

Our forefathers believed the fig contained the true elixir of life. Plato called the plant "the philosopher's friend." Meditate on the tree or fruit to acquire wisdom, improve your intuitive abilities, and become fertile in body and mind.

Lucky Bamboo (*Dracaena sanderiana*). This tropical indoor plant is not a true bamboo but looks like one due to its tall stalks. As the stalks grow, they can be braided together to form eye-catching, intertwined spirals that resemble a trunk. The only special requirement for this plant is to be kept in bright, diffuse light. Because it is native to tropical swamps, it can be grown hydroponically submerged in a dish of distilled water. Don't let the water get murky and rancid, as this will kill the plant. Freshen the water every week and don't bother with extra watering.

The lucky bamboo receives its name because feng shui practitioners affirm it makes both home and office vibrate with positive energy by stimulating chi. By tradition, a plant with two stalks confers good luck and love. Three stalks grant wealth, long life, and happiness. Meditate on lucky bamboo for prosperity, success in business, and joy.

Marjoram (*Origanum marjorana*). This perennial is tall for an herb, reaching up to three feet. It requires sun to partial shade and light, moist alkaline soil. The tiny pale white or red flowers grow in clusters on spikes. The part used for both herbal medicine and cooking is the leaf. The taste is much like oregano with hints of sweetness and warmth. Marjoram flavors beer and some meat and Italian dishes. It combines well with thyme. The herb's light fragrance scents potpourris; the red flowers render a reddish-brown dye.

Drink an infusion of the leaves to help cure a headache, calm the nerves, and expel intestinal gas. Marjoram tea also settles a queasy stomach, especially if you're experiencing seasickness. Applied externally, an infusion calms the aches of arthritis and sprains.

People once believed that carrying a small bag of dried marjoram leaves on a journey would protect the traveler and bring financial gain on the road. The ancient Romans associated this herb with Mercury, the planet and god of communication. Therefore, they reasoned, marjoram could facilitate communication with elemental spirits. A fifteenth-century spell recommends tacking marjoram sprigs into the four corners of your bedroom to attract a lifelong mate. For this to be successful, they warn, you must renew your marjoram supply every month! Meditate on this herb to find a good way to mediate a domestic dispute and achieve a positive resolution. Another meditation topic is how to make your next travel experience fulfilling.

Money Tree, Guiana Chestnut (*Pachira aquatica*). This versatile indoor tropical tree is similar in form and function to the lucky bamboo. It is a plant of the mallow family that can grow to seven feet in a swamp but is also capable of being turned into a bonsai. Braid the spindly stems in the same fashion as the lucky bamboo and the trunk will become woody. Like the bamboo, the money tree enjoys filtered, bright light. Unlike fruit trees and many other indoor plants, this tree is relatively free from disease and insect infestation.

At the end of each stem, five leaves unfurl that have come to symbolize the five Chinese elements of nature. In feng shui it is considered a lucky tree to place in the fame, health, or wealth areas of the home in order to mobilize the chi in those corners. Meditate on the money tree to manifest a long-term desire or to make a dream come true.

Palms. Palms make alluring indoor selections that lend a graceful, flowing, tropical flair to the environment. They also remove most indoor pollutants, thereby improving the air quality. Among the many varieties suitable for inside the house are the areca palm (*Chrysalidocarpus lutescens*), the bamboo palm (*Chamaedorea seifrizii*), and the lady palm (*Rhapis excelsa*).

Because the palm has long been associated with the Holy Land, this tree has acquired many symbolic meanings, including resurrection, inner strength, fertility, immortality, triumph over adversity, and, most of all, peace. Meditate on any of those topics to find balanced energy within and understand a challenging situation from a broader perspective.

Rosemary (*Rosmarinus officinalis*). Rosemary is easily raised indoors if there is plenty of light. Outside, if left to its own devices in a mild climate, this herb will grow to shrub stature. My friend in Suffolk, England, has a rosemary bush standing outside her kitchen that must be five feet wide and five feet tall. The name of this tender perennial of the mint family means "sea dew," which refers to the fact that the plant flourishes in dry calcareous soil near the sea. Sailors can smell its refreshing resinous odor twenty miles from land. Naturally, the dark green needlelike leaves with silver undersides make a pleasant resinous home air purifier. The needles also exude a crisp aroma when burned as incense. Rosemary is an ingredient of many ancient Celtic recipes because it is one of the few incense-making plants that can be grown in Britain.

In herbal medicine rosemary is touted as a heart tonic. It also helps cure migraine headaches and fainting spells due to its clean medicinal scent. Ancient Roman bakers swore that bread baked on a bed of rosemary would cure a person of dizziness and revive the scent of smell. Rosemary essential oil helps stimulate hair growth. Add three or four drops to one ounce jojoba oil. Rub into your head and let it sit for thirty minutes before washing out. As a culinary ingredient, rosemary needles are added to breads and rolls in a manner similar to poppy seeds. The lemony-pine flavor also combines satisfyingly with chicken, pork, lamb, pizza, olive oil, and tomato sauce. Take care to use rosemary sparingly as the taste is quite pungent.

This herb symbolizes fidelity; as the age-old saying goes, "Rosemary is for remembrance." It was formerly the custom in Wales for people to remember the dead by carrying rosemary garlands to funerals and placing them on graves. In ancient Greece students wore rosemary sprigs in their hair to help them recall their lessons, thus associating rosemary with knowledge and wisdom. Rosemary also helps release anger and bind old emotional wounds. This plant discourages nightmares, purifies the atmosphere, and soothes the troubled spirit, so it makes an excellent plant for a bedroom sanctuary. Meditate on rosemary to improve memory, enhance self-development, and acquire serenity and wisdom.

Sage (*Salvia officinalis*). This outdoor perennial of the mint family is native to the Mediterranean. Sage grows up to three feet tall and displays grayish-green leaves and blue-violet flowers. Of the many species, the wild variety (*S. sclarea*), native to Colorado, imparts a distinctively fresh scent. Sage is not a fussy plant; it flourishes in uncultivated ground in moderate drought conditions. Many species exist and many plants are called sage, but not all are related to *Salvia*. Unrelated plants can be used in incense-making, potpourri, and sachets but, for the most part, they do not substitute well in cooking. Sage is a popular beverage tea and also flavors wine and ale. It is a familiar ingredient in poultry dressings.

The genus name for sage means "healthy," which shows how highly the leaves are regarded in folk medicine. Aromatherapists claim that if you apply sage or rosemary to your skin, it will regulate the capillary action and revitalize this organ. Prevent a cold by boiling sage leaves with lemon and honey and drinking the brew. This formula also brings down a fever and eases the soreness from tonsillitis. Sage is also claimed to prevent aging and confer wisdom. It is alleged to thrive or wither in the garden according to the fortunes of the property owners. Meditate on sage to make a wise decision.

Snake Plant, Mother-in-Law's Tongue (*Sansevieria trifasciata*). This striking indoor plant receives its name from the narrow, green, swordlike leaves that thrust vertically into the air. The only special care required is bright, diffuse light. Stick a pot of this botanical on a shelf, water when the soil dries out, and enjoy its exotic beauty without having to pamper it. Some feng shui practitioners claim that the snake plant attracts negativity because it is spiky. Other experts in the same field contend that this is precisely the reason for the plant's positive energy, because it helps protect the household. The concept is akin to the Western viewpoint toward the planet and ancient god of war, Mars. On one hand, the energy is combative; on the other, it is fiercely protective. Also, entwined snakes form the caduceus, the medical symbol for healing. Meditate on the snake plant when you feel vulnerable and need shelter, strong protection, and a helping hand, especially when it comes to your health. Because snakes shed their skin, the plant that bears its name may also be contemplated for renewal or to understand why it is time to move on. For more information on snakes, see the entry in the section on totems.

Spider Plant (*Chlorophytum comosum*). Here is another undemanding indoor plant from which you can reap many rewards. It is slow-growing, doesn't like full sun, and is not especially picky about water and temperature. Spider plants are often grown in hanging baskets where their long stems can arch over the top of the pot. The so-called spiders are plantlets that form at the ends of the stems and look like spiders. If you want to acquire more plants, snip off a plantlet and repot. Spider plants are praised for their ability to filter carbon dioxide and formaldehyde from the air.

Some people associate the spider plant with spiders and, by analogy, spider webs. The web, which spirals to a central point where this arachnid makes its lair, is seen as a personification of the universe. The spider is also considered a symbol of transmutation because it weaves its web in the same way human destiny is perceived to be entwined. Others believe the spider to be a symbol of industrious labor. As you gaze at your gracefully draping spider plant, you may choose to meditate on these concepts as well as on self-determination and cosmic protection. For more information on spiders, see the entry in the section on totems.

Strawberry (*Fragaria* genus). This familiar outdoor perennial reaches to a mere six to ten inches. It requires rich, moist, well-drained soil and full sun, although my plants do well in partial shade. The flowers display five white petals with yellow centers that transform into juicy red fruit. Use slices of the fruit as a garnish, add them to smoothies, juice them, and make strawberry desserts like tarts, jams, jellies, and pies.

Strawberry leaves are used in herbal medicine to make an infusion as a female tonic, astringent, diuretic, and laxative. To whiten your teeth, rub a combination of apple, raspberry, and strawberry juice on your teeth. Wait five minutes, then clean off the juice with a half teaspoon of baking soda in a six-ounce glass of water. This is so much more pleasant and tasty than using whitening chemicals in your mouth!

In times gone by, people thought the ambrosial scent of strawberry juice would attract good fairies and gnomes to protect the home. In the language of flowers, this herb signifies "perfect excellence." Meditate on a bowlful of strawberries to fire your imagination and improve your intuition.

Thyme (*Thymus vulgaris*). This indoor/outdoor perennial grows from two to twelve inches, depending on the variety. If you keep it inside, place the pot in a sunny window. Thyme enjoys a dry, lime-rich soil but dislikes overwatering. Plant the mini thyme variety between the stones on your patio to prevent weeds from popping up. It will also lend a sweet balsamic fragrance to the air.

The leaves are the part used in cooking. They taste pungent, but I improve the flavor by adding lemon balm or lemon verbena. Thyme adds a balsamic flavor to egg and fish dishes as well as cheeses and liqueurs. In my opinion, the lemon thyme variety is best for drinking. In herbal medicine the leaves are used as an expectorant and to expel gas from the digestive system. An infusion made from the leaves and applied externally is an antiseptic that kill crabs, lice, and fungal infections. Thyme helps destroy the microorganism that causes yellow fever.

In ancient Greece this herb was considered a symbol of courage, energy, and graceful elegance. In medieval Europe damsels embroidered an image of thyme on scarves along with a bee and gave them to their knights as emblems of bravery in battle. In folklore this plant is alleged to uplift the spirits, improve memory and concentration, protect a family's health, and aid astral travel. Meditate on thyme to recharge your batteries and muster the courage to forge ahead.

Umbrella Tree (*Schefflera actinophylla*). This indoor tree is named for the drooping fingers of its leaves that resemble umbrellas. As it hails from the dense tropical forest, the umbrella tree requires little direct sunlight and is content in a north-facing window. Keep the plant moist at all times, but don't let the water stagnate in the catchall dish. Check under the leaves frequently for mites, scale, and other pests. Umbrellas protect us from rain and sun, so, by analogy, a fitting meditation topic for this plant is protection. Since by tradition it is the responsibility of fathers to protect and provide for us, paternal figures—whether of this world or the spirit world—provide another suitable meditation subject.

Yarrow (*Achillea millefolium*). The perennial yarrow does best outdoors as it requires full sun and reaches to a height of three feet. In the wild it can be found in dry meadows and on mountainsides in relatively poor soil. The mainly white and yellow blooms form large clusters that can be dried for flower arrangements. I have been cultivating a red-flowered variety called 'Paprika' that doesn't spread as fast as the others. The leaves and flowers are the parts used but taste too astringent and strongly sage-like to be of much use in cooking. Nevertheless, a tea can be brewed and ingested to remedy a severe cold. If you're out in a meadow or on a mountain and come down with a terrible toothache, chew on yarrow leaves for the pain until you can get to the dentist. Ancient Highlanders and Greeks used to prepare an ointment from yarrow to staunch bleeding in the battlefield and cure cuts and bruises.

Instead of coins, yarrow sticks are sometimes used to cast the Chinese I-Ching method of divination. Meditate on yarrow to understand suffering and regain strength and perspective.

Yucca (*Yucca aloifolia, Y. brevifolia, Y. glauca, Y. gloriosa*) is a perennial desert plant that, like all other plants from this region, requires little water and fertilizer but many hours of bright sunlight. Over forty species of this evergreen exist. Yucca makes an interesting selection for a home or sanctuary with contemporary decor. Its woody stem forms a trunk with strap-like leaves that emerge in groups of three at staggered heights. This plant can grow tall, so you need to cut off the top half as it outgrows the pot or it's likely to poke through the ceiling!

Native Americans have long valued this plant for practical reasons. It is edible, although the taste seems to be an acquired one. Yucca can be sliced and prepared like French fries, mashed with garlic, or combined with black beans and plantain, to name just a few of the dishes. Since it is tough and fibrous, Native Americans of the Southwest have woven baskets and sandals from it for centuries. Besides fiber, yucca contains vitamins C and K, folate, and antioxidants to boost the immune system. Scientists have isolated the antiinflammatory components of this plant and currently are using them to treat heart failure, Parkinson's, and Alzheimer's. Mashed and applied externally, yucca will soothe rashes, sores, and wounds. Concepts associated with yucca suitable for meditation include purification, transmutation, and family and clan ties.

Flowers

Fresh flowers can make a welcome addition to your sanctuary. Few of us fail to feel uplifted by these colorful beauties. In general, flowers symbolize happiness, joy, prosperity, good luck, fulfillment, a carefree period, honors, wishes fulfilled, beauty, springtime, renewal, love, and marriage—not to mention the lovely fragrances the blossoms impart!

If you can't afford to festoon your haven with fresh bouquets, you can still enjoy their perfume by purchasing an inexpensive aroma diffuser and adding a couple drops of floral essential oil for your meditation session. Alternatively, spread a single drop of essence on a light bulb, turn on the lamp, and let the heat diffuse the scent. Or cut a small branch from a flowering tree or bush and place it in a vase of water. Failing that, a bowl of edible fruit like cherries or apples makes a good substitute, and you can munch the fruit during your contemplations!

Here is a list of some familiar flowers and their meanings that can be used as meditation topics:

Apples/Apple Blossom. Goals to achieve, motherhood, temptation, thirst for knowledge.

Carnation. Fidelity, gentle love, motherhood, spirituality. The carnation is the official Mother's Day flower.

Chamomile. Humility, patience, perseverance in the face of adversity.

Cherry/Cherry Blossom. Continuing education, sensuality, social adaptability.

Chrysanthemum (Mums). Devotion, long life, loyalty, optimism, return of joy, exuberant yang energy.

Daffodil. Courtesy, friendship, hope, respect, success, wealth.

Daisy. Childhood, first love, innocence, naiveté, new beginnings, purity, shared secrets.

Dandelion. Growth, healing, making dreams come true, overcoming emotional pain, pride.

Geranium. Calmness, gentility, peace, tension reduction, yin/yang balance.

Heliotrope. Devotion, eternal love, prayer, prophecy, unity.

Hibiscus. Delicate beauty, harmony, stillness.

Honeysuckle. Happiness, lasting affection, union.

Iris. Admiration, respect, romance, valor, wisdom.

Jasmine. Creativity, love, sensuality, success, upliftment.

Lavender. Grounding and centering, healing, heightened awareness, inheritance, kinship, vitality, youth.

Lilac. Grace, hope, spirituality, spring love.

Lily. Happiness, health, soul's rebirth, remembrance of those who have moved or passed away.

Lily of the Valley. Chastity, childhood and early memories, magic, trustworthiness.

Lotus Blossom. Beauty, divinity, eloquence, femininity, fertility, self-realization.

Marigold. Blessings, consolation, departed souls, protection, return of happiness.

Orange/Orange Blossom. Directed and positive energy, harmony, health, peace, positive and directed energy, love, tranquility.

Pansy. Cheerfulness of mind, companionship, reflection, thoughtfulness.

Poppy. Empathy, imagination, peace, pleasure, sleep issues, wartime remembrances.

Rose. Aspirations, beauty, children, joy, love, perfection, popularity, romance, upliftment. The rose is a mood elevator that stimulates the heart chakra.

Sunflower. Blessings of nature, boldness, happiness, longevity, loyalty, strength.

Thistle. (Yes, the thistle has a pretty purple flower!) Bravery, determination, devotion, durability, strength, survival.

Tulip. Forgiveness, passion, perfect love, worthiness.

Violet. Abundance, breaking down barriers of indifference, calming strife, healing, moderation, modesty.

Gemstones

Healing properties have been ascribed to gemstones for centuries. While some people are skeptical that rocks can exert influences on physical reality, no one disputes their power to bedazzle. Gemstones can be displayed in the home for their beauty, to repel or attract certain energies, and as reminders of qualities for which to strive.

Here are a few appropriate meditation topics associated with some celebrated gems.

Agate. Polishes conversation skills, sharpens wits, instills courage and vitality, and confers a long, happy life.

Alexandrite. Synthesizes knowledge, strengthens the aura and self-esteem, and inspires creativity and independent thought.

Amber. Protects and creates a friendly, sensual environment. Burn the resin like incense to disinfect and fumigate.

Amethyst. Symbolizes friendship, vibrates compassion, encourages moderation, helps a person rise above day-to-day annoyances, and clears a troubled mind. Also nurtures creativity and helps produce prophetic dreams.

Aquamarine. Nurtures harmony in the home, cultivates individualism, restores composure after trying incidents, and stimulates a blissful love life. Calms stress in those of nervous dispositions. This gem of the ocean wanderer, mystic, and seer is said to refine intuitive abilities.

Aventurine. The Chinese "stone of heaven" enables a peaceful environment where inspiration can occur, especially for writing.

Bloodstone. Sometimes called hematite, heliotrope, or jasper. Allegedly confers courage, constancy, endurance, good health, and happiness.

Carnelian. An opaque and colorful stone that helps suppress fear, anger, melancholy, and an overactive imagination. A grounding stone that supports family unity and spiritual upliftment.

Chalcedony. Neutralizes negative thoughts, creates an environment conducive to an introspective frame of mind, and improves a sour disposition.

Chrysoberyl (Cat's Eye). Helps one gain insights into personal faults. Along with tiger's eye and hawk's eye (variations), it stimulates an independent spirit and advances business interests. All the "eyes" are alleged to enable the intuitively inclined to see both the past and the future.

Chrysoprase. A stone that calms nerves, balances the personality, and forges links to greenery, growth, and beginnings. A mind-expanding stone that helps promote fresh insights.

Citrine. Counterbalances negative thoughts, stabilizes the emotions, attracts transformative energy, helps one think sensibly about life, and inspires love of humanity.

Coral. Protects, confers wisdom, and arouses sexual attraction. I suggest keeping a specimen on your altar as a reminder that coral polyps are now endangered; see chapter 14 for details.

Diamond. Symbols of beauty, strength, and power, diamonds are esteemed by those who wish to perfect their inner beings and attain cherished goals. Beware: this stone is reputed to magnify *all* personality traits, both positive and negative.

Emerald. Balances the personality, facilitates communication, increases cerebral capacities, enflames passion, and strengthens resolve. Aids contemplation of the mysteries of creation.

Fluorite. Heals relationships, facilitates concentration, and fosters communication.

Garnet. Inculcates sentiments of courage, fortitude, and devotion. Draws good health, eliminates feelings of fear and guilt, and fires ambition. In folk tradition garnets are alleged to help a widow find a new mate, hence its sobriquet "the consolation stone."

Jacinth. Enables one to see the truth hidden beneath the surface and use intuition to avoid accidents and natural disasters such as flood, fire, tornado, earthquake, and tsunami.

Jade. Restores tranquility, inspires courage, confers wisdom, and foments self-esteem by unveiling one's inner beauty. To the Chinese, the chief among many of jade's virtues is to confer wisdom.

Jasper. This "marital" stone encourages constancy and everlasting passion in a long-term relationship. Also confers wisdom, courage, and good luck.

Jet. Stands for spiritual strength, which is one reason many rosaries are carved from it.

Lapis Lazuli. Kindles love and fidelity, strengthens the will, dispels melancholy, aids self-realization, calms nervous personalities, and improves communicative abilities.

Magnetite/Lodestone. Since this iron oxide literally can be attracted by a magnet, in folk tradition it is alleged to draw a variety of influences, from love to money and protection. The naturally dark gray stone is usually painted different colors to correspond to these uses, and then is sprinkled with iron filings that stick to the stone to prove it is magnetite.

Malachite. Helps humans decipher the language of animals, cultivates empathy with pets, elevates the spirits, and induces a restful night's sleep.

Moonstone. It is alleged that if you hold a moonstone in your mouth during the full moon, you will attract prosperity and good luck, and the path to take in the future will become clear.

Obsidian. A natural smooth glass used for centuries by cultures worldwide (the Aztecs being the most famous) as a visioning stone to open the third eye and enhance intuition. In contemporary times this stone has been a conduit for past-life recall.

Onyx. Hones listening skills, improves concentration, calms fear, and spurs renewal.

Opal. A so-called prophecy stone that awakens the senses, cultivates contact with the spirit world, and improves memory. Gem healers believe that since this gem vibrates on an intensely high energy level, it should not be worn by those with nervous dispositions.

Pearl. Improves the quality of the skin, calms the nerves, and purifies the body.

Peridot. Facilitates research and problem solving, symbolizes enjoyment of innocent and modest pleasures, attracts friends, and energizes the body. Also allays fears and pangs of homesickness.

Quartz. Volumes could and have been written about the virtues of this multitalented stone, of which only a few virtues can be mentioned here. A clear quartz crystal makes an ideal choice for those seeking to invigorate their personal spaces. Quartz is also used as a tool to fire the imagination, open the intuitive centers, and heal illness. Early Christians saw in this stone a symbol of the Immaculate Conception. The pink-hued rose quartz, a gentle variety, helps balance those of sensitive natures and calms the overly passionate.

Ruby. Purifies the air, strengthens the heart, inspires action, arouses energetic creativity, and cultivates independent thought. Also motivates procrastinators, helps a person act on the courage of convictions, and banishes melancholy.

Sapphire. Inspires devotion, spiritual enlightenment, and high aspirations. Enables peace of mind, furthers friendships, and helps one achieve independence. Induces clear vision and insight.

Topaz. Develops leadership, creativity, wisdom, and nobility. Builds trust, furthers friendships, and confers happiness.

Tourmaline. A consummate meditation stone that creates goodwill, joy, and self-confidence. Also assists understanding others and repels negativity. Folklore maintains that this gem is a lucky charm for performers, artists, and writers.

Turquoise. Protects, helps the possessor withstand melancholy, nurtures peace in the home, and relieves marital tension. Also enhances understanding of life's truths. This gem's color is especially conducive to meditation.

Numbers

Although it is possible to keep any number of items in your sanctuary, some people like to vary their displays according to the season, their mood, or their intentions. For example, you might place a single crystal on your altar to symbolize the New Year or when you wish to create a new beginning. You might light six candles to remind yourself to do six things to help others through a particularly trying time. As you read in the feng shui chapter, you may prefer to display items in pairs to enhance chi and bring good luck. I don't expect you'll ever put twenty-two items in your private space, which is the last number on the list, but you might want to draw this number on a sheet of colored construction paper and place it on your altar to remind you of an ideal you yearn to master.

Here are some traditional meanings for numbers:

0. Completion, loss.

1. The self, independence, strength, beginnings, self-reliance, freedom, leadership.

2. Union, second chance, change of residence, partnership, parenting, domestic life.

3. Joy, creativity, new skills, short journeys, friends, relatives, romance, short trips.

4. Gain, achievement, security, discipline, organization, health, home, real estate.

5. Conflict, foreign affairs, legal matters, letting go, adaptability, new paths.

6. Harmony, perfection, beauty, responsibilities, creativity, justice, health, pets.

7. Analysis, wisdom, public image, hidden influences, authority figures.

8. Ambition, renewal, sudden change, finances, efficiency, courage, power.

9. Romance, wish fulfillment, spiritual assistance, addiction, inspiration, foreign influences.

10. Acceptance, perseverance, marriage, home, dominion.

11. Change, stress, vision, idealism, inspiration.

12. Special talents, success, time to rest and regroup.

13. A demanding time, transformation.

14. Temperance, balance, spiritual growth, karma.

15. Focus, achievement, durability, the physical world, need to rise above material world.

16. Willpower, obstacles to overcome, wisdom, transitions, radical changes.

17. That which is hidden beneath the surface, good luck, occult forces afoot.

18. Receptivity, intuition, knowledge of the hidden, unconventionality.

19. Self-determination, link to universal life, energy, cosmic knowledge, collective intelligence.

20. Patience, diplomacy, relationships, judgment, new beginnings.

21. Creativity, fulfillment, victory, versatility, joy, victory, great spiritual masters.

22. Practical idealism, success, mastery, involvement in humanitarian and/or global pursuits.

Totems

Following is a list of animal totems. Their meanings may help you choose an animal spirit guide with whom to communicate and bond in your sanctuary. Animal totems also provide topics for meditation and contemplation.

Alligator/Crocodile. Longevity, adaptation, efficiency, facing fears.

Ant. Hard work for gain, thrift, successful partnerships.

Bat. Protection, longevity, happiness, introspection.

Bear. Wisdom, comfort, receptivity, safe haven, the supernatural, the subconscious, rebirth.

Bee. Diligence, domestic bliss, busyness, hard work, cooperation, prosperity, public success.

Beetle. Creation, transformation, renewal, fortitude, eternal life.

Bull. Creativity, fertility, strength, masculinity, decisiveness, the will.

Butterfly. Transformation, enjoyment of life, scattered thoughts, transitions.

Camel. Fortitude, wealth.

Cat. Independence, development of intuitive abilities, inner guidance.

Chicken. Industriousness.

Cock. Independence, self-confidence.

Cow. Beauty, creation, fertility, peace of mind, nourishment, pathfinding.

Coyote. Entertainment, issues needing study from multiple viewpoints.

Crab. Many-sided issues.

Crane. Diligence, fertility, springtime of life.

Crow/Raven. Messages, changes in consciousness, refined intelligence.

Deer. Gentleness, grace, nourishment, gratitude.

Dog. Companionship, loyalty, the guiding light, protection, tenacity.

Dolphin. Recovery from an illness, reward, salvation, evolution, the life force.

Donkey. Patience, self-sacrifice, inheritance.

Dove. Peace, the Holy Spirit, sadness, mourning, sacrifice, transformation of the soul.

Dragonfly. Balance of mind and spirit, awakenings, visions.

Duck. Fidelity, financial success, good luck.

Eagle. Power, fame, fertility, imagination, divine majesty, opportunity, the power of prayer.

Elephant. Cooperative spirit, divinity, service, eternity, leadership, love, moderation, wisdom.

Fish. Salvation, good fortune, abundance, marital happiness, success, productivity.

Fox. Eloquence, self-expression, intelligence.

Frog. Creativity, transformation, fertility, abundance, leap of faith.

Goat. Determination, persistence, courage.

Goose in Flight. Success, a carefree retirement.

Gull. Survival.

Hare/Rabbit. Fertility, growth, lunar influences, vigilance.

Hawk. Alertness, observation, a higher view.

Hen. Domestic bliss, housewifery.

Heron. Intuition, organizational skills.

Horse. Inner strength, beneficial change, freedom, grace, fertility, immortality, purpose.

Hummingbird. Adaptability, optimism, lightness of being, clarity, balance, resilience, matters of the hearth and health.

Kangaroo. Harmony, fast progress.

Lion. Ambition, prosperity, the performing arts, regeneration, decisions.

Otter. Playfulness, creativity, cooperation, priorities.

Owl. Truth, wisdom, patience, intuition, the mysteries of the universe.

Ox. The cosmic forces at work, self-sacrifice, patience, what lies deep within earth.

Parrot. The tropics, communications, new ideas.

Peacock. Riches, a prosperous estate, the incorruptible soul, resurrection of the body.

Pelican. Freedom, nobility, reflection.

Pig/Boar. Action, good fortune, financial success, growth, wildness, vitality.

Snakes (Intertwined). Healing, prophecy, medical science, vitality, immortality, spiritual riches.

Spider. Industriousness, self-determination, cunning, persistence, good luck.

Squirrel. Thrift, hard work, honesty, resourcefulness, abundance.

Swan. Beauty, contentment, mysticism, everlasting love, intuitive understanding of music.

Tiger. Boundaries, passion, vigor.

Tortoise/Turtle. Ancestors, creativity, achievement of aims, memory, the earth.

Whale. The Akashic Records, resounding success, motherhood, the collective unconscious.

Wolf. Ancestors, bravery, guidance, partnerships, self-reliance.

Trees

You have already met some tropical and fruit trees that can fit well into your sanctuary decor. Following are descriptions of trees whose wood makes superb choices for flooring, wall paneling, and furniture. All can be planted outdoors in most hardiness zones.

Ash (*Fraxinus* genus). Ash is a moderately priced tough and elastic hardwood used to fashion spears, bows, and oars. The color varies from creamy white or gray to dark reddish brown. Its flexible wood makes bent furniture parts that require a good deal of strength. Ash is a fine treehouse tree if the specimen is healthy. As of this writing, many ash trees in my home state of Colorado are being destroyed due to emerald ash borer infestation. Do not plant ash near other trees, as they strangle the others' roots with their suckers. Ash bark is both a tonic and astringent. Brew a tea from the bark and leaves to help cure jaundice and arthritis.

Since the ash is the famous tree from which Odin, the father god of Norse myth, is said to have hung to gain knowledge of the runes, it is associated with rebirth and wisdom. These make worthy meditation subjects, along with new beginnings and new projects. Other suitable topics include loyalty, reliability, and the ability to gain strength to obtain peace of mind.

Birch (*Betula* genus). Birch trees have beautiful foliage, which makes them handsome botanicals to plant in the garden. The hardwood has a pleasing grain and light yellowish-brown wood that resembles maple. Birch is useful for making furniture as well as canoes. The oil from the inner bark softens leather and lends a masculine scent to Russian leather perfume. Mix the essential oil with a carrier oil like jojoba and apply topically as an astringent and antiseptic to relieve sore muscles. Since birch bark was once used as a kind of paper for writing, you can meditate on this tree to improve your communication skills or finish a writing project.

Fir (*Abies* genus). Fir is a serviceable wood for building, especially for floors. It provides a strong home for a treehouse, except the lowest branches are usually flimsy. To use fir as a treehouse, you need a tall ladder or perhaps should select a tree that has another tree or several trees growing close to it for support. Turpentine, which is extracted from the wood and resin, thins paint and in a pinch cleans ulcers and wounds. The needles are an ingredient in herbal medicine to cure lung infections. Silver fir contains diuretic properties.

This tree is linked to childbirth and motherhood because it is the first day of the first month in the ancient Celtic tree calendar. Meditate on fir for new beginnings, conception, and to understand the responsibilities of motherhood.

Mahogany (*Swietenia macrophylla*). This strong tropical hardwood is treasured for crafting furniture, veneers, and carvings. The color is medium-brown to deep reddish-brown and dark red and has a handsome, distinctive grain. Mahogany is expensive, largely because it has been overharvested. The spiritual properties of this tree include healing the emotions and spirit. Having a representation of this wood in your sanctuary, even if it is a small carving, can provide guidance to help you grow spiritually.

Maple (*Acer* genus). The maple is much admired for its stellar beauty at any time of year but is especially striking in the fall when the changing leaves put on a show of brilliant color. It is a favorite shade tree for city and town streets across America. Maple makes a durable treehouse tree. Maple wood is so tough it is used for bowling alley flooring. The wood is highly prized in furniture-making for its light brown color with a reddish cast and grain that is usually straight but also occurs in bird's-eye, curling, and swirling patterns. This wood readily accepts any type of stain or paint, so you can paint it to match the rest of your decor.

Maple is such a useful tree. It supplies fuel wood and charcoal. The sap of the sugar maple, when confected into sugar candies or syrup, delights children of all ages. In addition, the bark is an astringent. A decoction of the leaves alleviates sore and bloodshot eyes. Meditate on this tree to understand the true meaning of inner beauty and open a line of communication with Spirit. Plant this tree outdoors; as it matures, you, too, shall learn and grow.

Spruce (*Picea* genus). Thirty-five species of this fast-growing, long-lived, medium softwood tree exist. My spruce is over one hundred years old, which is really saying something in this harsh, dry climate. However, my tree has no patch on one Norwegian spruce in Sweden said to be over 9,500 years old. Long, broad spruce branches sweep to the ground in perfect symmetry and provide shelter for wildlife. The spruce can also anchor a treehouse, but be aware that the roots are shallow. The leaves and branches make spruce beer, and the wood provides paper and soundboards for various musical instruments. Keywords associated with this tree are generosity, peace, and protection. These topics make good themes for meditation.

Walnut (*Juglans* genus). Walnut is a favorite squirrel tree. The nuts, so difficult to separate from the hard shell, are this rodent's epicurean delight. The leaf juice will dye the skin brown. This very strong but expensive hardwood is a popular choice for fine furniture and veneers. The wood is chocolate brown, sometimes with dark or purplish streaks but is also attainable in lighter shades. This makes walnut furniture a good choice for almost anybody's decor. If you build a treehouse, avoid locating it in a black walnut tree, as the branches snap easily.

Walnut is an astringent, detergent, and laxative. A decoction of the leaves ameliorates eczema, and the kernels cure wounds, carbuncles, and gangrene. It also makes a black ink. Meditate on walnut to ensure the success of new projects and escape from the negative influences of others.

Resources

This bibliography is arranged by general topic for easy access.

Clutter

Arnold, Jeanne E. *Life at Home in the Twenty-First Century: 32 Families Open Their Doors.* Cotsen Institute of Archaeology Press, 2012.

Consumer Reports. "The Best Ways to Sell Your Stuff." http://www.consumerreports.org/cro/magazine/2004/og/the-best-ways-to-sell-your-stuff/index.htm.

Doland, Erin Rooney. *Unclutter Your Life in One Week.* Gallery Press, 2010.

Druckerman, Pamela. "The Clutter Cure." *New York Times,* February 17, 2015.

Fels, Anna. "Why We Save the Remnants of Our Lives." *New York Times,* October 26, 2017.

Good Housekeeping Magazine. *Organize Your Home!* Hearst Communications, Time Inc. Books, 2017.

Kondo, Marie. *The Life-Changing Magic of Tidying Up: The Japanese Art of Decluttering and Organizing*. Ten Speed Press, 2014.

Magnusson, Margareta. *The Gentle Art of Swedish Death Cleaning: How to Free Yourself and Your Family from a Lifetime of Clutter*. Scribner, 2018.

Wallman, James. *Stuffocation: Why We've Had Enough of Stuff and Need Experience More Than Ever*. Spiegel & Grau, 2013.

Walsh, Peter. *Lighten Up: Love What You Have, Have What You Need, Be Happier with Less*. Free Press, 2011.

Gardens, Botanicals, and Trees

Bordman, Aileen. *Everyday Monet: A Giverny-Inspired Gardening and Lifestyle Guide to Living Your Best Impressionist Life*. Dey Street, 2018.

Chongue, Jason. *Plant Society: Create an Indoor Oasis for Your Urban Space*. Hardie Grant, 2018.

Conway, D. J. *By Oak, Ash, & Thorn: Modern Celtic Shamanism*. Llewellyn Publications, 1995.

Evelyn, Nancy. *The Herbal Medicine Chest*. Crossings Press, 1986.

Fourwords. *Miniature Terrariums: Tiny Glass Container Gardens Using Easy-to-Grow Plants and Inexpensive Glassware*. Tuttle, 2018.

Hayman, Richard. *Trees: Woodlands and Western Civilization*. Hambledon and London, 2003.

Hurwitz, Jane. *Butterfly Gardening: The North American Butterfly Association Guide*. Princeton University Press, 2018.

Logee's Plants for Home and Garden: Fruiting, Rare and Tropical Plants Catalog. Logee's Greenhouses, Fall 2017 Catalog.

McCulloch, Janelle. *Gardens of Style: Private Hideaways of the Design World*. Rizzoli, 2018.

Mettler, Lynn. "The World's 30 Best Treehouse Hotels." June 26, 2018. https://travel.usnews.com/gallery/the-worlds-30-best-treehouse-hotels.

Murray, Liz, and Conrad Murray. *The Celtic Tree Oracle: A System of Divination*. St. Martin's Press, 1988.

Musgrave, Toby. *Green Escapes: The Guide to Secret Urban Gardens*. Phaidon, 2018.

Nelson, Peter. *New Treehouses of the World*. Abrams, 2009.

Orlando, Richard. *Weeds in the Urban Landscape: Where They Come From, Why They're Here, and How to Live with Them*. North Atlantic Books, 2018.

Powers, Richard. *The Overstory*. W. W. Norton & Company, 2018.

Rohde, Eleanour Sinclair. *The Old English Herbals*. Dover, 1989.

"Spirit Garden Design." https://spiritgardendesign.com.

"Tree Symbolism: Ancient and Mystical Teachings." https://www.universeofsymbolism.com/tree-symbolism.html

Webster, Richard. *Flower and Tree Magic*. Llewellyn, 2008.

Weiseman, Wayne, Daniel Halsey, and Bryce Ruddock. *Integrated Forest Gardening: The Complete Guide to Polycultures and Plant Guilds in Permaculture Systems*. Chelsea Green Publishing, 2014.

Gemstones, Numbers, Planets, Talismans, and Totems

Ansel-Arieli, Melody. "Mezuzahs: Jewish Declarations of Devotion Enter the Realm of Collectibles." August 28, 2018. https://www.antiquetrader.com/antiques/mezuzahs-jewish-declarations-of-devotion-enter-the-realm-of-collectibles/.

Budge, E. A. Wallis. *Amulets and Talismans*. Collier Books, 1970.

Dow, Caroline. *Tea Leaf Reading for Beginners: Your Fortune in a Tea Cup*. Llewellyn, 2011.

Frazier, Gregory, and Beverly Frazier. *The Bath Book*. Troubador Press, 1973.

Hunt, Victoria. *Animal Omens*. Llewellyn, 2008.

Mager, Stefan. *Crystal Gemstone & Minerals Guide*. Llewellyn, 2017.

Mella, Dorothee L. *Stone Power*. Warner Books, Time Warner, 1988.

Morwyn. *Green Magic: The Healing Power of Herbs, Talismans, & Stones*. Schiffer, 2000.

Pavitt, William Thomas, and Kate Pavitt. *The Book of Talismans, Amulets, and Zodiacal Gems*. Tower Books, 1971.

Regardie, Israel. *The Art of True Healing*. New World Library, 1997.

Thompson, Robert Farris. *Face of the Gods: Art and Altars of Africa and the African Americas*. Museum for African Art, 1993.

Universe of Symbolism. Search this site for meanings of
animals, colors, flowers, numerology, and spiritual tools.
https://www.universeofsymbolism.com.

Uyldert, Mellie. *The Magic of Precious Stones*. Borgo
Press,1986.

Webster, Richard. *Amulets and Talismans for Beginners: How to
Choose, Make, and Use Magical Objects*. Llewellyn, 2004.

Home Decoration and Lifestyle

Alexander, Jane. *Spirit of the Home: How to Make Your Home a Sanctuary.* Thorsons, 1998. Other similar titles by the same author: *Spirit of the Living Room, Spirit of the Bedroom, Spirit of the Kitchen.*

Angelo, Jill. *Sacred Space: Turning Your Home into a Sanctuary.* CreateSpace, 2013.

Ariana. *House Magic: The Good Witch's Guide to Bringing Grace to Your Space.* Conari Press, 2001.

Birren, Faber. *Color Psychology and Color Therapy: A Factual Study of the Influence of Color on Human Life.* McGraw-Hill, 1950.

Bruchac, Joseph. *The Native American Sweat Lodge: History and Legends.* Crossing Press, 1993.

Collins, Josephine. *Your Home as a Sanctuary.* Ryland Peters & Small, 2004.

Deason, Tina Riddle. "Time for Myself." *SageWoman* no. 93, 2018.

DeSalle, Rob. *Our Senses: An Immersive Experience.* Yale University Press, 2018.

Gaynor, Elizabeth, Kari Haavisto, and Darra Goldstein. *Russian Houses.* Stewart, Tabori & Chang, 1991.

Lee. Vinny. *Coming Home: Spiritual Interiors.* Watson-Guptill Publications, 2002.

McGarvie, Irene. *The Sweat Lodge Is for Everyone.* Ancient Wisdom, 2009.

Morris, Tisha. *Decorating with the Five Elements of Feng Shui.* Llewellyn, 2015.

Postel-Vinay, Danielle. *Home Sweet Maison: The French Art of Making a Home.* HarperCollins, 2018.

St. Clair, Kassia. *The Secret Lives of Color.* Penguin, 2017.

Streep, Peg. *Altars Made Easy: A Complete Guide to Creating Your Own Sacred Space.* HarperSanFranciso, 1997.

Tidbury, Jane. *Zen Style: Balance and Simplicity for Your Home.* Universe, 1999.

Tudhope, Hilton. *Home for Health: Creating a Sanctuary for Healing.* Build for Health Press, 2018.

Webster, Richard. *Color Magic for Beginners.* Llewellyn, 2006.

West, Rebecca. *Happy Starts at Home: Getting the Life You Want by Changing the Space You've Got.* Bright House, 2016.

Williams, Nathan. *The Kinfolk Home: Interiors for Slow Living.* Artisan, 2015.

Wong, Angi Ma. *Feng Shui Dos and Taboos.* Storey Publishing, 2000.

Workman, Katie. "Fall's a Great Season to Create a 'Cabinet of Curiosities.'" October 4, 2017. https://apnews.com/2959108948bd4f6bb9edaa661ad90bdc.

Incense

Cunningham, Scott. *Complete Book of Incense, Oils, & Brews.* Llewellyn Publications, 2002.

Harding, Jennie. *Incense: Create Your Personal Blends of Incense to Enrich and Discover Your Sacred Inner Spaces.* Polair, 2005.

Morwyn. *Witch's Brew: Secrets of Scents.* Schiffer, 2000.

Neal, Carl F. *Incense: Crafting and Use of Magickal Scents.* Llewellyn, 2003.

Sacred Sites

Daley, Ben. *The Great Barrier Reef: An Environmental History.* Routledge, 2014.

"Environmental Threats to the Great Barrier Reef." https://en.wikipedia.org/wiki/Environmental_threats_to_the_Great_Barrier_Reef.

Marshall, Steve. *Exploring Avebury: The Essential Guide.* The History Press, 2016.

McCalman, Iain. *The Reef: A Passionate History.* Farrar, Straus and Giroux, 2014.

Parker Pearson, Michael. *Stonehenge: A New Understanding: Solving the Mysteries of the Greatest Stone Age Monument.* The Experiment, 2013.

Sobol, Laurel Marie. *Iguazu Falls National Park Gallera Journal.* CreateSpace, 2016.

Index

Baths, 74, 98, 104

    A Healing Bath, 104

    Inner Guide Oil Blend, 106, 107

    Roman Baths at Caracalla, 98

    Serenity Bath Bag, 105

    Solve a Problem Bath, 107

Bedrooms, 4, 5, 22, 23, 25, 27, 31, 56, 57, 60–64, 66, 69, 74, 98, 108, 111, 129, 130, 168, 209, 210, 223, 224, 268, 271, 303

Beloved Community Village, 175

Boundaries, 2, 134, 136, 292

Brazil Vitaminas, 36

Buddhist, 21

Budget, 62, 114, 116, 160, 209, 219, 237, 247

Butterfly Houses, 218

Cabinets of Curiosities, 304

Cacti, 55, 56, 63, 168, 187

Campbell, Joseph, 1

Celtic Hole Stones, 139

Chanumpa, 217

Chi, 45–54, 56, 58, 168, 184,
     188, 250, 268, 269, 287

Chinese, 13, 21, 43, 52, 121, 133,
     138, 215, 269, 276, 282, 284

Chromotherapy, 37

Cliff Palace, 251

Clutter, 3, 47, 61, 146, 149, 154,
     155, 158, 162, 297, 298

Decluttering Memory Clutter, 154

Color
     Color Healing, 14, 21, 37–40, 304
     Color Palette, 20
     Color Psychology, 28, 30, 32, 34, 303
     Complementary Colors, 19, 22–24,
          26–28, 37, 72
     Color Meanings, 32, 234, 302

Condos, 147, 152, 165, 167, 168, 171

Culture Shock, 233

Debugging, 220, 221

Dikenga, 232

Dorm Rooms, 169